LIVING LANGUAGE®

COMPLETE ITALIAN

THE BASICS

REVISED & UPDATED

COMPLETE ITALIAN

THE BASICS

REVISED & UPDATED

REVISED BY LORRAINE-MARIE GATTO

Based on the original

by Genevieve A. Martin

and Mario Ciatti

LIVING LANGUAGE

Published in the United States by Living Language, A Random House Company

www.livinglanguage.com

Editor: Zviezdana Verzich
Production Editor: Jacinta O'Halloran
Production Manager: Heather Lanigan
Interior Design: Sophie Ye Chin

ISBN 1-4000-2141-3

Library of Congress Cataloging-in-Publication Data available upon request.

This book is available for special discounts for bulk purchases for sales promotions or premiums. Special editions, including personalized covers, excerpts of existing books, and corporate imprints, can be created in large quantities for special needs. For more information, write to Special Markets/ Premium Sales, 1745 Broadway, MD 6-2, New York, NY, 10019 or e-mail specialmarkets@randomhouse.com.

Printed in the United States of America
10 9 8 7 6 5 4 3 2 1

CONTENTS

INTRODUCTION

Living Language® Complete Italian: The Basics makes it easy to learn how to speak, read, and write Italian. In this course, the basic elements of the language have been carefully selected and condensed into forty short lessons. If you can study about thirty minutes a day, you can master this course and learn to speak Italian in a few weeks.

This *Complete Italian: The Basics* provides English translations and brief explanations for each lesson. The first five lessons cover pronunciation, laying the foundation for learning the vocabulary, phrases, and grammar that are explained in the later chapters. If you already know a little Italian, you can use the book as a phrase book and reference. In addition to the forty lessons, there is a Summary of Italian Grammar, plus verb conjugations, and a section on letter writing.

Also included in the course package is the *Living Language® Italian Dictionary*. It contains more than 15,000 entries, with many of the definitions illustrated by phrases and idiomatic expressions. More than 1,000 of the most essential words are capitalized to make them easy to find. You can increase your vocabulary and range of expression just by browsing through the dictionary.

Practice your Italian as much as possible, even if you can't manage a trip abroad. Watching Italian movies, reading Italian magazines, eating at Italian restaurants, and talking with Italian-speaking friends are enjoyable ways to help you reinforce what you have learned with *Complete Italian: The Basics*. Now, let's begin.

The following instructions will tell you what to do. *Buona fortuna!* Good luck!

COURSE MATERIAL

1. Two 90-minute cassettes or three 60-minute compact discs.

2. *Living Language® Complete Italian: The Basics*. This book is designed for use with the recorded lessons, but it may also be used alone as a reference. It contains the following sections:

   Basic Italian in 40 Lessons
   Summary of Italian Grammar
   Verb Conjugations
   Letter Writing

3. *Living Language® Italian Dictionary:* The Italian/English–English/Italian dictionary contains more than 15,000 entries. Phrases and idiomatic expressions illustrate many of the definitions. More than 1,000 of the most essential words are capitalized.

INSTRUCTIONS

1. Look at page 1. The words in **boldface** type are the ones you will hear on the recording.

2. Now read Lesson 1 all the way through. Note the points to listen for when you play the recording. The first word you will hear is **Alfredo.**

3. Start the recording, listen carefully, and say the words aloud in the pauses provided. Go through the lesson once and don't worry if you can't pronounce everything correctly the first time around. Try it again and keep repeating the lesson until you are comfortable with it. The more often you listen and repeat, the longer you will remember the material.

4. Now go on to the next lesson. If you take a break between lessons, it's always good to review the previous lesson before starting a new one.

5. There are two kinds of quizzes in the coursebook. With matching quizzes, you must select the English translation of the Italian sentence. The other type requires you to fill in the blanks with the correct Italian word chosen from the three given directly below the sentence. If you make any mistakes, begin again and reread the section.

6. There are 18 supplemental vocabulary sections in the course. Each one focuses on a useful theme that is usually related to the content of the surrounding lessons. Practice the lists through repetition, self-quizzes, or with flash cards to build a solid foundation in Italian vocabulary.

7. Even after you have finished the forty lessons and achieved a perfect score on the Final Quiz, keep practicing your Italian by listening to the recordings and conversing with Italian-speaking friends. For further

study, try *Complete Italian: Beyond The Basics,*
Ultimate Italian Beginner-Intermediate, Ultimate
Italian Advanced, Italian Without the Fuss, or *2,000+*
Italian Verbs, all from the experts at Living Language.
Or, go to our website at www.livinglanguage.com for
more information on the available Italian courses and
reference materials.

LIVING LANGUAGE®

COMPLETE
ITALIAN
THE BASICS

REVISED & UPDATED

LESSON 1

A. SOUNDS OF THE ITALIAN LANGUAGE

Many Italian sounds are similar to the English. Listen to and repeat the following Italian names, and notice which sounds are similar and which are different:

Alfredo	Alfred	**Luigi**	Louis
Antonio	Anthony	**Luisa**	Louise
Carlo	Charles	**Maria**	Mary
Caterina	Katherine	**Michele**	Michael
Enrico	Henry	**Paolo**	Paul
Elisabetta	Elizabeth	**Peppino**	Joe
Emanuele	Emanuel	**Pietro**	Peter
Ferdinando	Ferdinand	**Raffaele**	Raphael
Francesco	Francis	**Raimondo**	Raymond
Giovanni	John	**Riccardo**	Richard
Giorgio	George	**Roberto**	Robert
Giulia	Julia	**Rosa**	Rose
Giuseppe	Joseph	**Vincenzo**	Vincent
Isabella	Isabel	**Violetta**	Violet

NOTE:

1. That each vowel is pronounced clearly and crisply.

2. That a single consonant is pronounced with the following vowel.

3. That some vowels bear an accent mark, which sometimes shows the accentuated syllable:

la città   the city

but sometimes merely serves to distinguish words:

e   and   **è**   is

4. When the accent is on the letter *e*, it gives a more open pronunciation:

caffè   coffee

5. The apostrophe (') is used to mark elision, the omission of a vowel. For example, when the word *dove* (where) is combined with *è* (is), the *e* in *dove* is dropped: *Dov'è*? Where is?

Now listen to some geographical names:

Bari	**Napoli**
Brindisi	**Ravenna**
Genova	**Sardegna**
Legnano	**Sicilia**
Livorno	**Taranto**
Messina	**Urbino**
Milano	**Venezia**

Now the names of some countries:

Argentina	**Inghilterra**
Belgio	**Messico**
Cina	**Norvegia**
Spagna	**Giappone**
Stati Uniti	**Portogallo**
India	**Egitto**
Francia	**Venezuela**
Germania	**Russia**

B. COGNATES: WORDS SIMILAR IN ENGLISH AND ITALIAN

Now listen to and repeat the following cognates (words that are similar in English and Italian). Notice how Italian spelling and pronunciation differ from English:

azione	action	**certo**	certain
agente	agent	**chitarra**	guitar
attenzione	attention	**differente**	different
caso	case	**difficile**	difficult
centro	center	**esempio**	example

festa	feast	**ristorante**	restaurant
importante	important	**simile**	similar
interessante	interesting	**té**	tea
nazione	nation	**teatro**	theater
necessario	necessary	**telefono**	telephone
possibile	possible	**treno**	train
radio	radio	**visita**	visit

LESSON 2

A. THE ITALIAN ALPHABET

LETTER	NAME	LETTER	NAME	LETTER	NAME
a	*a*	h	*acca*	q	*qu*
b	*bi*	i	*i*	r	*erre*
c	*ci*	l	*elle*	s	*esse*
d	*di*	m	*emme*	t	*ti*
e	*e*	n	*enne*	u	*u*
f	*effe*	o	*o*	v	*vu*
g	*gi*	p	*pi*	z	*zeta*

B. PRONUNCIATION PRACTICE WITH COGNATES

The following groups of cognates will give you some additional practice in Italian pronunciation and spelling:

attore	actor	**generoso**	generous
animale	animal	**generale**	general
capitale	capital	**umore**	humor
centrale	central	**locale**	local
cereale	cereal	**materiale**	material
cioccolato	chocolate	**originale**	original
colore	color	**personale**	personal
dottore	doctor	**probabile**	probable
familiare	familiar	**regolare**	regular

simile	similar	**totale**	total
semplice	simple	**usuale**	usual

LESSON 3

A. VOWELS

1. *a* is like *ah,* or the *a* in *father:*

a	to, at	**lago**	lake
amico	friend *(masc.)*	**pane**	bread
la	the *(fem.sing.)*[1]	**parlare**	to speak

2. *e* is like the *e* in *cent:*

era	was	**treno**	train
essere	to be	**tre**	three
pera	pear	**estate**	summer
padre	father	**se**	if
carne	meat		

e in the middle of a word may have two different sounds when stressed:

OPEN SOUND		CLOSED SOUND	
me	me	**verde**	green
e	and	**venti**	twenty
tre	three	**tema**	fear

---

[1] *fem.sing.* stands for *feminine singular.* In Italian, nouns are either masculine or feminine, and the words that modify them agree in gender and number (singular or pural).

3. *i* is like the *i* in *police, machine, marine,* but not
   drawled:

misura	measure	**oggi**	today
sì	yes	**piccolo**	small *(masc.sing.)*
amica	friend *(fem.)*	**figlio**	son

4. *o* is like the *o* in *no,* but not drawled:

no	no	**con**	with
poi	then	**otto**	eight
ora	hour	**come**	how
sono	am, are	**forma**	form
corpo	body	**voce**	voice

5. *u* is like the *u* in *rule,* but not drawled:

uno	one *(masc.)*	**tu**	you *(fam.)*[1]
una	one *(fem.)*	**ultimo**	last

6. Notice that each vowel is clearly pronounced, and that
   Italian vowels tend to be shorter and crisper than
   English vowels:

Europa	Europe	**poesia**	poem
leggere	to read	**creare**	to create
dov'è	where is	**mio**	my
io sono	I am	**paese**	country
idea	idea		

---

[1] Italian distinguishes between familiar and polite forms of "you." The *tu* form is reserved for children, close friends, relatives, and pets. Use the *Lei* form, which is more polite, when addressing people you have just met, as well as with professionals and others you wish to show respect for.

B. Diphthongs: Double Vowel Combinations

1. *ai:*

guai	troubles		

2. *au:*

aula	room	**autunno**	autumn

3. *ei:*

sei	six	**dei**	of the

4. *eu:*

Europa	Europe	**neutro**	neutral

5. *ia:*

Italia	Italy	**patria**	homeland

6. *ie:*

piede	foot	**tieni**	(you) keep

7. *io:*

stazione	station	**piove**	it is raining

8. *iu:*

fiume	river	**piuma**	feather

9. *oi:*

poi	then	**noi**	we

10. *ua:*

quale	what	**quattro**	four

11. *ue:*

questo	this	**quello**	that

12. *ui:*

buio	darkness	**lui**	him

13. *uo:*

buono	good	**tuo**	your (*fam.*)

C. TRIPHTHONGS: TRIPLE VOWEL COMBINATIONS

1. *iei* (pronounce: yeh-ee):

miei   my

2. *iuo* (pronounce: you-oh):

figliuolo   son

3. *uoi* (pronounce: woe-ee):

tuoi   your *(fam.)*

LESSON 4

A. CONSONANTS

1. *b* is pronounced like the English *b* in *boat*:

bottiglia   bottle

2. *c* has two different sounds:

before *a, o, u*, it is equivalent to the English *k* in *bake:*

caso   case

before *e* or *i* it is equivalent to the English *ch* in *church:*

celibe   bachelor

3. *d* is like the English *d* in *dark:*

data   date

4. *f* is equivalent to the English *f:*

forza   force

5. *g* has two different sounds: before *a, o, u*, it is equivalent to the English *g* in *go:*

guida   guide

before *e* or *i*, it is equivalent to the English *g* in *general*:

generoso   generous

6. *h* is not pronounced. It is found only in exclamations:

Ah!   Ah!

in certain forms of the verb *to have*:

io ho   I have

or in words of foreign origin:

hotel   hotel

7. *l, m, n, p* are equivalent to the corresponding letters in English:

libertà	liberty	**notte**	night
memoria	memory	**prova**	proof

8. *q* is used only in combination with *u* and is pronounced like the English *qu* in *quality*.

quarto   quarter

9. *r* is rolled, similar to Spanish pronunciation:

regione   region

10. *s* has two different sounds:

at the beginning of a word, when used double, or when followed by another consonant it is equivalent to the *s* in *song*:

sale	salt	**fresco**	cool
rosso	red		

when occurring between two vowels it sounds like a *z*:

causa	cause	**poesia**	poetry
esilio	exile		

11. *t, v* are equivalent to the corresponding letters in English:

tono	tone	**vacanza**	vacation

12. *z* has two different sounds:

harsh, as in the English combination *ts*. This sound generally occurs in the group *-zione*.

azione	action	**addizione** addition
nazione	nation	

soft, as in the English combination *ds*. This sound occurs mostly in technical and classical words derived from Greek.

zona	zone	**zebra**	zebra

B. SPECIAL ITALIAN SOUNDS

Pay special attention to the following sounds, which do not have exact English equivalents:

1. *cc* when followed by *i* or *e* is pronounced like the English *ch* in *chair:*

cacciatore	hunter	**faccia**	face

2. *ch* before *e* and *i* is pronounced like the English *k* in *key:*

chitarra	guitar	**chiodo**	nail

3. *gh* before *e* and *i* is pronounced like the English *g* in *gate:*

ghiaccio	ice	**ghetto**	ghetto

4. *gli* is always pronounced as one letter; the closest English approximation would be the combination *lli*, as in *million:*

figlia	daughter	**paglia**	straw
foglia	leaf	**giglio**	lily

5. *gn* is always pronounced as one letter, somewhat like the English *ni* in *onion,* or *ny* in *canyon:*

segno	sign	**Spagna**	Spain
montagna	mountain	**lavagna**	blackboard

6. *sc* before *e* and *i* is pronounced like the English *sh* in *shoe:*

scendere	(to) climb	**sciroppo**	syrup
scimmia	monkey	**scivolare**	(to) slip

7. *sc* before *a, o,* and *u* is pronounced like the English *sk* in *sky:*

scuola	school	**Scozia**	Scotland
scarpa	shoe	**scoiattolo**	squirrel

C. MORE ITALIAN-ENGLISH COGNATES

Building up an Italian vocabulary is fairly easy since a great number of words are similar in English and Italian. Some words are spelled exactly the same (though they may differ considerably in pronunciation):

ITALIAN	ENGLISH	ITALIAN	ENGLISH
antenna	antenna	**zoo**	zoo
area	area	**idea**	idea
auto	auto	**opera**	opera
radio	radio	**cinema**	cinema

There are many Italian words that you will have no difficulty in recognizing despite minor differences. Some of these differences are:

1. The Italian words add *e.*

annuale	annual	**origine**	origin
occasionale	occasional	**speciale**	special
parte	part		

2. The Italian words add *a* or *o.*

lista	list	**costo**	cost
problema	problem	**liquido**	liquid
persona	person		

3. The Italian words have *a* or *o* where the English ones have *e*.

causa	cause	**favorito**	favorite
figura	figure	**minuto**	minute
medicina	medicine	**tubo**	tube
rosa	rose	**uso**	use

D. General Spelling Equivalents

1. Italian *c (cc)* = English *k (ck)*:

franco	frank	**parco**	park
sacco	sack	**attacco**	attack

2. Italian *f* = English *ph:*

frase	phrase	**telefono**	telephone
fisico	physical	**fonico**	phonic

3. Italian *s (ss)* = English *x:*

esercizio	exercise	**Messico**	Mexico
esempio	example	**fisso**	fix

4. Italian *st* = English *xt:*

estensione	extension	**estremo**	extreme
esterno	external		

5. Italian *t* = English *th:*

autore	author	**teatro**	theatre
simpatia	sympathy	**teoria**	theory

6. Italian *z (zz)* = English *c:*

forza	force	**razza**	race

7. Italian *i* = English *y:*

stile	style	**sistema**	system
mistero	mystery	**ritmo**	rhythm

8. Italian *o* = English *ou:*

corte	court	**corso**	course
montagna	mountain		

9. Italian *-io* = English *-y:*

segretario	secretary	**territorio**	territory

10. Italian *-zione* = English *-tion:*

nazione	nation	**addizione**	addition

11. Italian *-o* = English *-al:*

interno	internal	**politico**	political
eterno	eternal		

12. Italian *-oso* = English *-ous:*

famoso	famous	**generoso**	generous
numeroso	numerous	**religioso**	religious

LESSON 5

A. NUMBERS 1–10

uno	one
due	two
tre	three
quattro	four
cinque	five
sei	six
sette	seven
otto	eight
nove	nine
dieci	ten

Uno più uno fa due.	One and one is two.
Uno più due fa tre.	One and two is three.
Due più due fanno quattro.	Two and two are four.
Due più tre fanno cinque.	Two and three are five.
Tre più tre fanno sei.	Three and three are six.
Tre più quattro fanno sette.	Three and four are seven.
Quattro più quattro fanno otto.	Four and four are eight.
Cinque più quattro fanno nove.	Five and four are nine.
Cinque più cinque fanno dieci.	Five and five are ten.

B. DAYS OF THE WEEK[1]

lunedì	Monday
martedì	Tuesday
mercoledì	Wednesday
giovedì	Thursday
venerdì	Friday
sabato	Saturday
domenica	Sunday

C. MONTHS OF THE YEAR

gennaio	January
febbraio	February
marzo	March
aprile	April
maggio	May
giugno	June
luglio	July
agosto	August
settembre	September
ottobre	October
novembre	November
dicembre	December

[1] The names of the days of the week and of the months are never capitalized.

D. SEASONS

primavera	spring
estate	summer
autunno	autumn
inverno	winter

E. NORTH, SOUTH, EAST, WEST

nord	north
sud	south
est	east
ovest	west

F. MORNING, NOON, AND NIGHT

mattina	morning
mezzogiorno	noon
pomeriggio	afternoon
sera	evening
notte	night

G. TODAY, YESTERDAY, TOMORROW

oggi	today
ieri	yesterday
domani	tomorrow

Oggi è venerdì.	Today is Friday.
Ieri era giovedì.	Yesterday was Thursday.
Domani è sabato.	Tomorrow is Saturday.

H. COLORS

rosso	red
blu	blue

verde	green
nero	black
bianco	white
giallo	yellow
bruno	brown
marrone	brown (coffee color)
grigio	gray

QUIZ 1

Try matching these two columns:

1. *venerdì*	a. January
2. *autunno*	b. summer
3. *giovedì*	c. June
4. *primavera*	d. winter
5. *otto*	e. October
6. *gennaio*	f. white
7. *inverno*	g. autumn
8. *verde*	h. Sunday
9. *giugno*	i. eight
10. *estate*	j. spring
11. *lunedì*	k. west
12. *quattro*	l. Thursday
13. *ottobre*	m. four
14. *domenica*	n. ten
15. *ovest*	o. red
16. *rosso*	p. black
17. *nero*	q. green
18. *dieci*	r. Friday
19. *bianco*	s. gray
20. *grigio*	t. Monday

ANSWERS

1—r; 2—g; 3—l; 4—j; 5—i; 6—a; 7—d; 8—q; 9—c; 10—b; 11—t; 12—m; 13—e; 14—h; 15—k; 16—o; 17—p; 18—n; 19—f; 20—s.

LESSON 6

A. GREETINGS

DI MATTINA	IN THE MORNING
buon	good
giorno	morning (day)[1]
Buon giorno.	Good morning.
Signor	Mr.
Rossi.	Rossi.
Buon giorno, signor Rossi.	Good morning, Mr. Rossi.
Salve	Hello *(pol.)*
Ciao	Hello/Good-bye *(fam.)*
come	how
sta	are you
Come sta?	How are you? How do you do? *(pol.)*
Come stai?	How are you? *(fam.)*
molto	very
bene	well
Molto bene.	Very well.
grazie	thank you, thanks
Molto bene, grazie.	Very well, thank you.
E Lei?[2]	And you? *(pol.)*
E tu?	And you? *(fam.)*
bene	fine
Bene, grazie.	Fine, thank you.
Arrivederci.	Good-bye.
Ciao.	Bye. *(fam.)*

[1] Words in parentheses are literal translations.
[2] Italian has both a polite, formal form of "you" *(Lei)* and an informal, familiar form *(tu)*. Use *tu* when talking to family, good friends, pets or children. In other situations, it's better to err on the side of politeness and use *Lei*.

DI SERA	IN THE EVENING
buona	good
sera	evening
Buona sera.	Good evening.
Buona sera, signora Rossi.	Good evening, Mrs. Rossi.
Buona notte.	Good night.
Buona notte, signorina Rossi.	Good night, Miss Rossi.

Note: The Italian word for "sir" or "Mr." is *signore,* but when it is used immediately preceding a name, the *e* is dropped.

Buon giorno, signor Rossi.
Buon giorno, signore.

B. How's the Weather?

Che tempo fa oggi?	What's the weather today?
Fa bel tempo.	It's nice (beautiful weather).
Fa brutto tempo.	It's awful (ugly weather).
Fa freddo.	It's cold.
Fa fresco.	It's cool.
Fa caldo.	It's hot.
Piove.	It's raining.
Nevica.	It's snowing.
C'è il sole.	It's sunny.
È nuvoloso.	It's cloudy.
Tira vento.	It's windy.

QUIZ 2

1. *mattina*
2. *signora*
3. *E Lei?*
4. *molto bene*
5. *Buon giorno.*

a. Good evening.
b. How are you? *(pol.)*
c. Miss
d. morning
e. Thank you.

6. *Buona notte.*	f. Madam or Mrs.
7. *Come sta?*	g. How are you? *(fam.)*
8. *Piove.*	h. sir or Mr.
9. *Grazie.*	i. What's the weather today?
10. *Come stai?*	j. Good morning.
11. *signorina*	k. It's nice.
12. *Buona sera.*	l. And you? *(pol.)*
13. *Che tempo fa oggi?*	m. very well
14. *signore*	n. It's raining.
15. *Fa bel tempo.*	o. Good night.

ANSWERS

1—d; 2—f; 3—l; 4—m; 5—j; 6—o; 7—b; 8—n; 9—e; 10—g; 11—c; 12—a; 13—i; 14—h; 15—k.

C. WORD STUDY

classe	class
considerabile	considerable
differenza	difference
elemento	element
gloria	glory
operazione	operation
madre	mother
padre	father

SUPPLEMENTAL VOCABULARY 1: WEATHER

it's raining	*piove*
it's snowing	*nevica*
it's hailing	*grandina*
it's windy	*c'è vento, tira vento*
it's hot	*fa caldo*
it's cold	*fa freddo*

it's sunny	*c'è il sole*
it's cloudy	*è nuvoloso*
it's beautiful	*fa bello*
storm	*il temporale*
wind	*il vento*
sun	*il sole*
thunder	*il tuono*
lightening	*il lampo*
hurricane	*l'uragano*
temperature	*la temperatura*
degree	*il grado*
rain	*la pioggia*
snow	*la neve*
cloud	*la nuvola*
fog	*la nebbia*
smog	*lo smog*
umbrella	*l'ombrello*

LESSON 7

A. WHERE IS . . . ?

dove	where
è	is
dov'è *(dove è)*	where is
Dov'è un albergo?	Where is a hotel?
buon ristorante	good restaurant
Dov'è un buon ristorante?	Where's a good restaurant?
dov'è	where is
Dov'è?	Where is it?
Dov'è il telefono?	Where's the telephone?
Dov'è il ristorante?	Where's the restaurant?

Dov'è la toilette?	Where's the bathroom?
Dov'è la stazione?	Where's the train station?
Dov'è l'ufficio postale?	Where's the post office?

B.   CAN YOU TELL ME . . . ?

può dirmi[1]	can you tell me *(pol.)*
Può dirmi dov'è un albergo?	Can you tell me where there is a hotel?
Può dirmi dov'è un buon ristorante?	Can you tell me where there is a good restaurant?
Può dirmi dov'è il telefono?	Can you tell me where the telephone is?
Può dirmi dov'è la stazione?	Can you tell me where the train station is?
Può dirmi dov'è l'ufficio postale?	Can you tell me where the post office is?

QUIZ 3

1. *Dov'è un albergo?*	a. Where's the telephone?
2. *Dov'è il telefono?*	b. Can you tell me where the train station is?
3. *Può dirmi Lei . . . ?*	c. Can you tell me . . . ?
4. *Può dirmi dov'è la stazione?*	d. the post office
5. *l'ufficio postale*	e. Where is a hotel?

ANSWERS
1—e; 2—a; 3—c; 4—b; 5—d.

---

[1] Note that the question *Può dirmi . . . ?* (Can you tell me?) can be used with or without the pronoun *Lei.*

C. DO YOU HAVE . . . ?

Ha . . . ?	Do you have . . . ? *(pol.)*
Hai . . . ?	Do you have . . . ? *(fam.)*
denaro	(any) money
sigarette	(any) cigarettes
fiammiferi	(any) matches

Ho bisogno di . . .	I need . . .
carta	(some) paper
una matita	a pencil
una penna	a pen
un francobollo	a stamp
dentifricio	toothpaste
un asciugamano	a towel
sapone	soap

Dove posso comprare . . . ?	Where can I buy . . . ?
un dizionario italiano	an Italian dictionary
un dizionario inglese-italiano	an English-Italian dictionary
un libro in inglese	an English book
degli abiti	some clothes

D. IN A RESTAURANT

(prima) colazione	breakfast
pranzo	lunch
cena	dinner
Che cosa desidera?	What will you have? (What do you wish?)
Che cosa desidera mangiare?	What would you like to eat?
Mi dia il menu, per favore.	Give me the menu, please.
Posso avere il menu, per favore?	May I have the menu, please?

Mi porti . . .	Bring me . . .
un po' di pane	some bread
della minestra	some soup
della carne	some meat
del manzo	some beef
una bistecca	a steak
del prosciutto	some ham
del pesce	some fish
del pollo	some chicken
delle uova	some eggs
della verdura	some vegetables
delle patate	some potatoes
dell'insalata	some salad
dell'acqua	some water
del vino	some wine
della birra	some beer
del latte	some milk
un caffè latte	coffee with milk
dello zucchero	some sugar
del sale	some salt
del pepe	some pepper
della frutta	some fruit
dei dolci	some dessert

Mi porti . . .	Bring me . . .
una tazza di caffè	a cup of coffee
una tazza di tè	a cup of tea
un tovagliolo	a napkin
un cucchiaio	a spoon
un cucchiaino	a teaspoon
un coltello	a knife
un piatto	a plate
un bicchiere	a glass

Desidero . . .	I would like . . .
un po' di frutta	some fruit (assorted)
una bottiglia di vino	a bottle of wine

un' altra bottiglia di vino	another bottle of wine
un po' di più	a little more
un po' più di pane	a little more bread
un po' più di carne	a little more meat

Il conto, per favore. The check, please.

QUIZ 4

1. *carne*
2. *patate*
3. *acqua*
4. *Che cosa desidera?*
5. *uova*
6. *pollo*
7. *pesce*
8. *una bottiglia di vino*
9. *Ho bisogno di sapone.*
10. *Mi porti un po' più dì pane.*

11. *caffelatte*
12. *zucchero*
13. *verdura*
14. *una tazza di tè*

15. *un piatto*
16. *un coltello*
17. *dolci*
18. *prima colazione*
19. *un cucchiaio*
20. *Il conto, per favore.*

a. fish
b. water
c. vegetables
d. I need soap.
e. The check, please.
f. breakfast
g. a spoon
h. coffee with milk
i. What will you have?
j. dessert

k. meat
l. a knife
m. eggs
n. Bring me a little more bread.

o. chicken
p. a cup of tea
q. a plate
r. sugar
s. a bottle of wine
t. potatoes

ANSWERS

1—k; 2—t; 3—b; 4—i; 5—m; 6—o; 7—a; 8—s; 9—d; 10—n; 11—h; 12—r; 13—c; 14—p; 15—q; 16—l; 17—j; 18—f; 19—g; 20—e.

SUPPLEMENTAL VOCABULARY 2: FOOD

dinner	*la cena*
lunch	*il pranzo*
breakfast	*la colazione*
meat	*la carne*
chicken	*il pollo*
beef	*il manzo*
pork	*il maiale*
veal	*il vitello*
fish	*il pesce*
shrimp	*il gambero*
lobster	*l' aragosta*
bread	*il pane*
egg	*l' uovo (m.), le uova (f. pl.)*
cheese	*il formaggio*
rice	*il riso*
vegetable	*la verdura*
lettuce	*la lattuga*
tomato	*il pomodoro*
zucchini	*lo zucchino*
eggplant	*la melanzana*
carrot	*la carota*
cucumber	*il cetriolo*
pepper	*il peperone*
fruit	*la frutta*
apple	*la mela*
orange	*l' arancia*
banana	*la banana*
pear	*la pera*
peach	*la pesca*
apricot	*l' albicocca*
grapes	*l' uva*
drink	*la bevanda*
water	*l' acqua*

milk	*il latte*
juice	*il succo*
coffee	*il caffè*
tea	*il tè*
wine	*il vino*
beer	*la birra*
soft drink / soda	*la bibita*
salt	*il sale*
pepper	*il pepe*
sugar	*lo zucchero*
honey	*il miele*
hot/cold	*caldo/freddo*
sweet/sour	*dolce/amaro*

LESSON 8

A. To Speak: *PARLARE*

io parlo	I speak
tu parli	you speak *(fam.)*
lui parla	he speaks
lei parla	she speaks
Lei parla	you speak *(pol.)*
noi parliamo	we speak
voi parlate	you speak *(plur.)*
loro parlano	they speak *(masc. or fem.)*
Loro parlano	you speak *(formal plur.)*

NOTES

1. These forms, which make up the present tense, translate into the English as "I speak," "I am speaking," and "I do speak." *Parlare* is an *-are* verb (also called a verb

of the first conjugation) because its infinitive form (to speak) ends in *-are*. There are many other common *-are* verbs that are conjugated like *parlare:*

lavorare	to work	**mangiare**	to eat
studiare	to study	**cucinare**	to cook

2. *Tu,* you, is used to address people you know very well (whom you call by their first names in English—relatives, close friends, children, pets, etc.). The plural for *tu* is *voi. Lei,* you, is used to address people you're meeting for the first time or don't know very well, acquaintances, superiors, and elders. The plural for *Lei* is *Loro,* but in conversation you will probably hear *voi* used as the plural for both *tu* and *Lei.*

3. Notice that there are six endings that indicate the person speaking or spoken about, without need of pronouns:

Singular:
    -o indicates the speaker (I)
    -i indicates the person spoken to (you). It is used only with someone you know well.
    -a indicates someone or something spoken about (he, she, it), or else you *(pol.).*

Plural:
    -iamo indicates several speakers (we).
    -ate is the plural form for *tu. Voi* is also used to address one or more persons in a polite way.
    -ano indicates they (both masculine and feminine). *Loro* is also used to address one or more persons in a formal way.

4. Notice that the verb form with *Lei, lui, lei* is the same: *parla.*

5. Notice that *lui* or *lei* is used with the verb form *parla,* depending on whether you are referring to a man or a woman:

lui parla   he is speaking
lei parla   she is speaking

6. The subject pronouns *lei, loro,* and the direct object pronouns *le, la, li* when they mean "you" are often capitalized to emphasize the idea of respect toward a person—for instance, when writing a formal letter or addressing someone in a respectful way. They are capitalized in this program for clarity.

B. THE AND A

1. The

MASCULINE

Singular: Plural:

il libro   the book   **i libri**   the books
lo studio   the study   **gli studi**   the studies
l'esercizio   the exercise   **gli esercizi**   the exercises

FEMININE

Singular: Plural:

la donna   the woman   **le donne**   the women
l'agenzia   the agency   **le agenzie**   the agencies

Notice the different forms used in Italian for the single English word *the.* In Italian, words are either masculine or feminine. When they refer to males or females, you know which group of articles to use, but in the case of other nouns, you have to learn whether the noun is masculine or feminine. The masculine article *il* and its plural form *i* are used before masculine nouns beginning with a consonant. The masculine article *lo* and its plural form *gli* are used before masculine nouns beginning with a vowel or a *z,* or *s* plus another consonant, or the consonant combination *gn.* When used before a vowel, *lo* is elided to *l';* the plural does not elide unless the following word begins with an *i*. The feminine article *la* and its plural form *le* are used before feminine nouns; however, before vowels, *la* is also elided to *l'*.

2. A (An)

MASCULINE		FEMININE	
un ragazzo	a boy	**una ragazza**	a girl
uno zero	a zero	**un'amica**	a friend *(fem.)*

The indefinite article (a, an) has the form *un* before masculine nouns beginning with vowels and most consonants. It takes the form *uno* before masculine nouns beginning with *z*, or *s* plus another consonant, or the combination *gn*. The feminine form is *una*, eliding to *un'* before a vowel.

QUIZ 5

1.	*io*	a.	they speak
2.	*noi*	b.	she is speaking
3.	*tu parli*	c.	she
4.	*lui*	d.	you *(plur.)*
5.	*loro parlano*	e.	I
6.	*voi*	f.	you speak
7.	*tu*	g.	he
8.	*lei*	h.	we speak
9.	*noi parliamo*	i.	you *(fam. sing.)*
10.	*lei parla*	j.	we

ANSWERS

1—e; 2—j; 3—f; 4—g; 5—a; 6—d; 7—i; 8—c; 9—h; 10—b.

C. CONTRACTIONS

di + il = del (of the)	*a + il = al* (to the)
di + lo = dello	*a + lo = allo*

di + la = della
di + l' = dell'
di + i = dei
di + gli = degli
di + le = delle

a + la = alla
a + l' = all'
a + i = ai
a + gli = agli
a + le = alle

con + il = col (with the)
con + i = coi

su + il = sul (on the)
su + la = sulla
su + lo = sullo
su + gli = sugli

D. PLURALS OF NOUNS

As a general rule, nouns ending in *o* are masculine, nouns ending in *a* are feminine, and nouns ending in *e* can be either masculine or feminine.

All masculine nouns (ending either in *o* or *e*) form their plural with an *i*.

Feminine nouns that end in *a* in the singular form their plural with an *e*. Feminine nouns that end in *e* in the singular form their plural with an *i*.

il piatto	the plate	**i piatti**	the plates
il cuore	the heart	**i cuori**	the hearts
la rosa	the rose	**le rose**	the roses
la valle	the valley	**le valli**	the valleys

E. ADJECTIVES

There are two groups of adjectives:

1. Those that have four endings:

caro *(masc. sing.)*
cari *(masc. plur.)*

cara *(fem. sing.)*
care *(fem. plur.)*

2. Those that have only two endings:

gentile *(masc. and fem. sing.)*
gentili *(masc. and fem. plur.)*

Study these examples:

un caro amico	a dear friend *(masc.)*
una cara amica	a dear friend *(fem.)*
dei cari amici	some dear friends *(masc.)*
delle care amiche	some dear friends *(fem.)*
un uomo gentile	a kind man *(masc.)*
una donna gentile	a kind woman *(fem.)*
degli uomini gentili[1]	some kind men *(masc.)*
delle donne gentili[1]	some kind women *(fem.)*

The adjective always agrees with its noun. When an adjective is used alone, its ending usually tells you whether it refers to a singular or plural, feminine or masculine noun:

È italiano.	He is Italian.
È italiana.	She is Italian.
Sono italiani.	They are Italian.
Sono italiane.	They are Italian. *(fem.)*

NOTES

Only proper names and geographical nouns are capitalized in Italian. Names of nationalities are not capitalized.

Examples:

un libro italiano	an Italian book
Ho incontrato un italiano.	I met an Italian.
Loro parlano italiano.	They speak Italian.

---

[1] Note that some adjectives come before the noun they modify, and some after. See Section 9 in the Summary of Italian Grammar.

F. POSSESSION

English -'s or -s' is translated by *di* (of):

il libro di Giovanni	John's book (the book of John)
i libri dei ragazzi ·	the boys' books (the books of the boys)
il libro di Maria	Maria's book
i libri delle ragazze	the girls' books

G. ASKING A QUESTION

To ask a question you can either put the subject after the verb:

Ha mangiato Lei?	Have you eaten?

or preserve the same word order and raise your voice at the end of the sentence to show that it is a question. Compare:

Lei ha mangiato.	You have eaten./You ate.
Lei ha mangiato?	Have you eaten?/Did you eat?

H. NOT

The word for "not" is *non*. It comes before the verb.

Non vedo Marco.	I don't see Mark.
Non sono italiana.	I'm not Italian.

REVIEW QUIZ I

1. *Buon* _____ (morning), *signora Rossi*.
    a. *domani*
    b. *giorno*
    c. *grazie*
2. *Può dirmi* _____ (where's) *l'ufficio postale?*
    a. *dov'è*
    b. *buono*
    c. *lì*

3. _____ (Bring me) *un po' di pane.*
   a. *Mangiare*
   b. *Sera*
   c. *Mi porti*
4. *caffelatte con* _____ (sugar)
   a. *tè*
   b. *vino*
   c. *zucchero*
5. *un po'* _____ (more) *di carne*
   a. *più*
   b. *tazza*
   c. *ancora*

6. *il sette* _____ (January)
   a. *marzo*
   b. *gennaio*
   c. *agosto*
7. _____ (Wednesday), *cinque settembre*
   a. *inverno*
   b. *sabato*
   c. *mercoledì*
8. _____ (How) *sta?*
   a. *Grazie*
   b. *Come*
   c. *Sera*
9. *Buona* _____ (evening), *signorina Rossi.*
   a. *fino*
   b. *sera*
   c. *io*
10. *Desidero una bottiglia di* _____ (wine).
    a. *latte*
    b. *vino*
    c. *acqua*

LESSON 9

A. MAY I INTRODUCE . . . ?

Buon giorno.	Good morning.
Buon giorno, signore.	Good morning, sir.
Come sta?	How are you? *(pol.)*
Molto bene, grazie e Lei? Lei E americano?	Very well, thanks, and how are you? Are you American?
Sì, signore.	Yes, sir.
Parla italiano?	Do you speak Italian?
Un po'.	A little.
La presento alla mia amica, signorina Rossi.	Let me introduce you to my friend, Miss Rossi.
Posso presentarLe la mia amica, signorina Rossi?	May I introduce my friend, Miss Rossi?
Molto piacere di conoscerLa.	Pleased to meet you. (Much pleasure in knowing you.)
Felice di conoscerLa.	I'm glad (happy) to meet (know) you.
Il piacere è mio.	The pleasure is mine.
Mi permetta che mi presenti: sono Giovanni Rossi.	Allow me to introduce myself: I'm John Rossi.

SUPPLEMENTAL VOCABULARY 3: PEOPLE

person	*la persona*
man	*l'uomo*

woman	*la donna*
adult	*l' adulto*
child	*il bambino/la bambina* (from 0 to 10 years old)
boy	*il ragazzino* (from 11 to 13), *il ragazzo* (from 14 to 35)
girl	*la ragazzina* (from 11 to 13), *la ragazza* (from 14 to 35)
teenager	*l' adolescente, teenager*
tall/short	*alto/basso*
old/young	*vecchio/giovane*
fat/thin	*grasso/magro*
friendly/unfriendly	*simpatico/antipatico*
happy/sad	*felice/triste*
beautiful/ugly	*bello/brutto*
sick/healthy	*malato/sano*
strong/weak	*forte/debole*
famous	*famoso*
intelligent	*intelligente*
talented	*con talento, in gamba* (colloquial)

B. HOW ARE THINGS?

Buon giorno, Paolo!	Hello, Paul!
Ciao, Giovanni!	Hi, John!
Come stai?	How are you? *(fam.)*
Come vanno le cose?	How are things? (How go things?)
Bene e tu?	Fine, and how are you? *(fam.)*
che c'è	what is there
di nuovo	(of) new
Che c'è di nuovo?	What's new?
niente	nothing
di particolare	in (of) particular
Niente di particolare.	Nothing in particular.

che	what
mi racconti	do (you) tell me
Che mi racconti?	What's new?
Poche cose.	(Few things.) Not much.
Non molto.	Not much.

C. Good-Bye

è stato	it's been
un vero piacere	a real pleasure
È stato un vero piacere.	It's been a real pleasure.
il piacere	the pleasure
Il piacere è stato mio.	The pleasure was mine.
Arrivederci ad un altro giorno.	Good-bye until another day.
A presto.	See you soon.
A più tardi.	See you later.
Buona notte.	Good night.
Ciao!	Good-bye/Hello. *(fam.)*
A dopo!	See you later!
Ci vediamo.	See you.
Alla prossima.	Until next (time).
A domani.	See you tomorrow.

QUIZ 6

1. *Come stai?*
2. *Arrivederci.*
3. *Buona notte.*
4. *Buon giorno, Giovanni.*
5. *Niente di particolare.*
6. *Mi permetta di presentarLa al mio amico.*
7. *A presto.*

a. Nothing in particular.
b. Allow me to introduce you to my friend.
c. See you soon.
d. Hello, John.
e. Pleased to meet you.
f. How are you?
g. Good night.

8. *nuovo*   h. to meet you
9. *Molto piacere di*   i. new
   conoscerLa
10. *conoscerLa*   j. Good-bye.

ANSWERS

1—f; 2—j; 3—g; 4—d; 5—a; 6—b; 7—c; 8—i; 9—e;
10—h.

LESSON 10

A. TO BE OR NOT TO BE: *ESSERE*[1]

Study these forms of the important irregular verb *essere,*
"to be."

io sono	I am
tu sei	you are *(fam.)*
Lei è	you are *(pol.)*
lui è	he is
lei è	she is
noi siamo	we are
voi siete	you are *(plur.)*
Loro sono	you are *(formal plur.)*
loro sono	they are
Lui è dottore.	He is a doctor.
Lui è scrittore.	He is a writer.
Lui è italiano.	He's Italian.
Il libro è rosso.	The book is red.
Lei è giovane.	She is young.

---

[1] See Section 43 of the Grammar Summary for more information about
essere.

Il ghiaccio è freddo.	Ice is cold.
Lui è intelligente.	He's intelligent.
Lei è incantevole.	She's charming.
Sono io.	It's me.
Di dov'è Lei?	Where are you from? *(pol.)*
Di dove sei?	Where are you from? *(fam.)*
Io sono italiano.	I'm Italian.
Di cosa è fatto?	What is it made of?
È fatto di legno.	It's made of wood.
È d'argento.	It's silver.
Di chi è questo?	Whose is this?
Il libro è del signor Rossi.	The book belongs to Mr. Rossi.
È l'una.	It's one o'clock.
Sono le due.	It's two o'clock.
Sono le nove e dieci.	It's ten past nine.
(Sono) otto euro la dozzina.	They are eight euros a dozen.
(Sono) cinque euro l'uno.	They are five euros each.
È tardi.	It's late.
È presto.	It's early.
È necessario.	It's necessary.
È un peccato.	It's a pity.
Non è vero?	Right? (Isn't it true?)

The verb *stare* means "to stay, to remain," but in certain expressions, such as expressions of health, it corresponds to the English verb "to be."

io sto	I stay (am)
tu stai	you stay (are)
lui sta	he stays (is)
noi stiamo	we stay (are)
voi state	you stay (are)
loro stanno	they stay (are)

Come sta?[1]   How are you? *(pol.)*
Sto bene.   I am well.

QUIZ 7

1. *Lui è intelligente.*	a. Whose is this?
2. *È un peccato.*	b. Where are you from?
3. *Lui è dottore.*	c. they are
4. *io sono*	d. He's a doctor.
5. *È l'una.*	e. It's early.
6. *noi siamo*	f. He's Italian.
7. *È fatto di legno.*	g. He's intelligent.
8. *Di dov'è Lei?*	h. It's a pity.
9. *È presto.*	i. I am
10. *Io sono stanco.*	j. It's one o'clock.
11. *loro sono*	k. It's made of wood.
12. *Di chi è questo?*	l. we are
13. *È tardi.*	m. I'm tired.
14. *Lui è italiano.*	n. It's late.

ANSWERS

1—g; 2—h; 3—d; 4—i; 5—j; 6—l; 7—k; 8—b; 9—e;
10—m; 11—c; 12—a; 13—n; 14—f.

B. IT IS . . .

È . . .   It is . . .
È vero.   It's true.
Questo non è vero.   This isn't true.
Questo non è così.   This isn't so.
È così. Così è.   It's so. That's the way it is.
È male.   It's bad.

---

[1] See Section 44 of the Grammar Summary for the verb *stare*.

È molto male.	It's very bad.
È certo.	It's certain.
È grande.	It's big.
È piccolo.	It's small.
È caro.	It's expensive.
È economico.	It's affordable.
È vicino.	It's near.
È lontano.	It's far.
È difficile.	It's difficult.
È facile.	It's easy.
È poco. Non è molto.	It's a little. It's not much.
È molto poco.	It's very little.
È molto.	It's a lot.
È abbastanza.	It's enough.
Non è abbastanza.	It's not enough.
È qui.	It's here.
È lì.	It's there.
È tuo.	It's yours. *(fam.)*
È Suo.	It's yours. *(pol.)*
È mio.	It's mine.
È nostro.	It's ours.
È per te.	It's for you. *(fam.)*
È per Lei.	It's for you. *(pol.)*

QUIZ 8

1. *È molto.*	a. It's enough.
2. *È facile.*	b. This isn't true.
3. *È vicino.*	c. It's bad.
4. *È abbastanza.*	d. It's near.
5. *Questo non è vero.*	e. It's mine.
6. *È male.*	f. It's true.
7. *È piccolo.*	g. It's here.
8. *È vero.*	h. It's small.
9. *È mio.*	i. It's easy.
10. *È qui.*	j. It's a lot.

1—j; 2—i; 3—d; 4—a; 5—b; 6—c; 7—h; 8—f; 9—e;
10—g.

C. To Have and Have Not: *Avere*

TO HAVE

io ho	I have
tu hai	you have *(fam.)*
Lei ha	you have *(pol.)*
lui ha	he has
noi abbiamo	we have
voi avete	you have
loro hanno	they have

NOT TO HAVE

io non ho	I don't have
tu non hai	you don't have *(fam.)*
Lei non ha	you don't have *(pol.)*
lui non ha	he doesn't have
noi non abbiamo	we don't have
voi non avete	you don't have
loro non hanno	they don't have

Study these expressions with *avere*.

Io ho tempo.	I have time.
Io non ho tempo.	I don't have any time.
Lui non ha amici.	He doesn't have any friends.
Ha una sigaretta?	Do you have a cigarette?

Io ho fame.	I'm hungry. (I have hunger.)
Ho sete. (Io ho sete.)	I'm thirsty. (I have thirst.)
Ho freddo. (Io ho freddo.)	I'm cold. (I have cold.)
Ho caldo. (Io ho caldo.)	I'm hot. (I have heat.)
Ho ragione.	I'm right. (I have reason.)

QUIZ 9

1. *noi abbiamo*	a. I'm cold.
2. *lui non ha*	b. we have
3. *Io non ho tempo.*	c. he doesn't have
4. *Ho freddo.*	d. I'm hungry.
5. *Io ho fame.*	e. I don't have time.

ANSWERS

1—b; 2—c; 3—e; 4—a; 5—d.

LESSON 11

A. I ONLY KNOW A LITTLE ITALIAN

1. *Parlare:* to speak

Parla italiano?	Do you speak Italian? *(pol.)*
Lei parla italiano?	Do you speak Italian? *(pol.)*
Sì, un po'.	Yes, a little.
Molto poco.	Very little.
Non molto bene.	Not very well.
Io parlo italiano.	I speak Italian.
Lo parlo male.	I speak it poorly.
Io non lo parlo molto bene.	I don't speak it very well.
Il suo amico parla italiano?	Does your friend speak Italian?

No, il mio amico non parla italiano.	No, my friend doesn't speak Italian.

2. *Conoscere:* to know; to be acquainted with

Io conosco solo poche parole.	I know only a few words.

3. *Leggere:* to read; *Dire:* to say

Lo leggo ma non lo parlo.	I read it, but I don't speak it.
Che cosa ha detto?	What did you say? *(pol.)*

4. *Capire:* to understand

Capisce l'italiano?	Do you understand Italian?
Sì, capisco l'italiano.	Yes, I understand Italian.
Lo capisco ma non lo parlo.	I understand it, but I don't speak it.
Lo leggo ma non lo parlo.	I read it, but I don't speak it.
No, io non capisco l'italiano.	No, I don't understand Italian.
Io non capisco molto bene l'italiano.	I don't understand Italian very well.
Non lo pronuncio molto bene.	I don't pronounce it very well.
Mi manca la pratica.	I lack practice.
Ho bisogno di pratica.	I need practice.
Lei mi capisce?	Do you understand me?
Io La capisco.	I understand you.
Io non La capisco molto bene.	I don't understand you very well.
Lei parla troppo in fretta.	You speak too fast. (You speak in too much of a hurry.)
Lei parla troppo veloce.	You are speaking too fast.
Non parli così in fretta.	Don't speak so fast. *(pol.)*
Parli più lentamente.	Speak more slowly. *(pol.)*

Per favore, parli più lentamente.	Please speak a little more slowly. *(pol.)*
Mi scusi ma non La capisco.	Excuse me, but I don't understand.
Non L'ho capita.	I didn't understand you.
Per favore me lo ripeta.	Please say it again (to me). *(pol.)*
Mi capisce ora?	Do you understand me now? *(pol.)*
Oh, ora capisco.	Oh, now I understand.

5. *Scrivere:* to write; *Significare:* to mean, to denote

Che cosa significa in italiano?	What does it mean in Italian?
Come si dice "Thanks" in italiano?	How do you say "Thanks" in Italian?
Come si scrive questa parola?	How do you spell (write) that word?
Per favore me la scriva.	Please write it down for me. *(pol.)*

B. A Brief Conversation with a Stranger

Buon giorno, signore.	Good morning, sir.
Buon giorno.	Good morning.
Lei parla italiano?	Do you speak Italian?
Sì, parlo italiano.	Yes, I speak Italian.
Non parlo inglese.	I don't speak English.
Lei è italiano?	Are you Italian?
Sì, sono italiano.	Yes, I am Italian.
Da quanto tempo è negli Stati Uniti?	How long have you been in the United States?
Da tre mesi.	For three months.
Imparerà presto l'inglese.	You'll soon learn English.

Imparerà l'inglese in poco tempo. Non è molto difficile.	You'll learn English in no time (little time). It's not very hard.
È più difficile di quanto creda.	It's harder than you think.
Forse ha ragione.	You are probably right.
È più facile per noi imparare l'italiano che per voi l'inglese.	It is easier for us to learn Italian than for you (to learn) English.
Lei parla italiano molto bene.	You speak Italian very well.
Ho vissuto in Italia per diversi anni.	I lived in Italy for several years.
Ha un'ottima pronuncia.	You have (an) excellent pronunciation.
Molte grazie, ma mi manca la pratica.	Thank you, but I need (lack) practice.
Ho bisogno di pratica.	I need practice.
Adesso devo andare. Il mio treno sta per partire.	I have to go now. My train's about to leave.
Buona fortuna e buon viaggio.	Good luck and have a nice trip.
Altrettanto.	The same to you.
Addio.	Farewell.

C. EXCUSE ME AND THANK YOU

Mi scusi.	Pardon me. Excuse me.
Le chiedo scusa.	I beg your pardon.
Per favore, ripeta.	Please repeat.
Mi vuole fare il favore di ripetere?	Will you do me the favor of repeating it?
Con piacere.	With pleasure. Gladly.
Con molto piacere.	With the greatest pleasure.
Sono a Sua disposizione.	I'm at your disposal.

Che cosa posso fare per Lei? What (thing) can I do for you?

Lei è molto gentile. You are very kind.

Lei è molto cortese. You are very kind. (You are very courteous.)

Grazie. Thanks.

Molte grazie. Many thanks.

Grazie infinite. Thanks a lot. (Infinite thanks.)

Mille grazie. Thanks very much. (A thousand thanks.)

Di niente. Don't mention it. (Of nothing.)

Non c'è di che. Don't mention it.

Prego. You're welcome.

QUIZ 10

1. *Lo comprendo ma non lo parlo.*
2. *Mi comprende ora?*
3. *Non lo parlo molto bene.*
4. *Lei è molto gentile.*
5. *Come si scrive questa parola?*
6. *Lei parla italiano?*
7. *Ho bisogno di pratica.*
8. *Non c'è di che.*
9. *Me lo ripeta.*
10. *Non molto bene.*
11. *Parli più lentamente.*
12. *Mille grazie.*

a. Do you speak Italian?
b. I need practice.
c. Don't mention it.
d. What did you say?
e. Say it again.
f. Not very well.
g. I didn't understand very well.
h. I understand it, but I don't speak it.
i. Speak more slowly.
j. I don't speak it very well.
k. How do you say "Thanks" in Italian?
l. You are very kind.

13. *Che cosa ha detto?*	m. Do you understand me now?
14. *Come si dice "Thanks" in italiano?*	n. How do you spell this word?
15. *Non ho capito bene.*	o. Thank you very much.

ANSWERS

1—h; 2—m; 3—j; 4—l; 5—n; 6—a; 7—b; 8—c; 9—e; 10—f; 11—i; 12—o; 13—d; 14—k; 15—g.

D. WORD STUDY

commedia	comedy
costante	constant
contrario	contrary
desiderio	desire
lungo	long
opera	opera
semplice	simple
venditore	vendor

LESSON 12

A. THIS AND THAT (DEMONSTRATIVE PRONOUNS AND ADJECTIVES)

Study the following expressions using the demonstratives *questo* and *quello*.[1]

Dammi questo.	Give me this one. *(masc.)*
Dammi questa.	Give me this one. *(fem.)*

[1] See also Section 21 in the Summary of Italian Grammar.

Dammi questi.	Give me these. *(masc.)*
Dammi queste.	Give me these. *(fem.)*
Dammi quello.	Give me that one. *(masc.)*
Dammi quella.	Give me that one. *(fem.)*
Dammi quelli.	Give me those. *(masc.)*
Dammi quelle.	Give me those. *(fem.)*
Dammi quello là.	Give me that one *(masc.)* over there.
Dammi quella là.	Give me that one *(fem.)* over there.
Dammi quelli là.	Give me those *(masc.)* over there.
Dammi quelle là.	Give me those *(fem.)* over there.

When *questo* and *quello* are used as adjectives preceding nouns, the forms of *questo* are the same as above, but *quello* has a different set of endings:

questo ragazzo	this boy
questa signora	this woman
quel signore là	that gentleman over there
quella signora	that woman
quello sbaglio	that mistake
quei vicini	those neighbors
quegli studenti	those students

QUIZ 11

1. *Dammi questi.*
2. *questo*
3. *Dammi quella.*
4. *questo ragazzo*
5. *quello*
6. *quei vicini*
7. *Dammi quelli là.*

a. Give me those over there.
b. that one over there
c. this woman
d. this one
e. that gentleman over there
f. this boy
g. Give me these.

8. *quello là*   h. that one
9. *questa signora*   i. those neighbors
10. *quel signore là*   j. Give me that one. *(fem.)*

ANSWERS
1—g; 2—d; 3—j; 4—f; 5—h; 6—i; 7—a; 8—b; 9—c; 10—e.

SUPPLEMENTAL VOCABULARY 4: AT HOME

house	*la casa*
apartment	*l'appartamento, l'alloggio*
room	*la camera, la stanza*
livingroom	*il soggiorno*
diningroom	*la sala da pranzo*
kitchen	*la cucina*
bedroom	*la camera da letto, la stanza da letto*
bathroom	*il bagno*
hall	*l'ingresso*
closet	*l'armadio*
window	*la finestra*
door	*la porta*
table	*il tavolo*
chair	*la sedia*
sofa/couch	*il divano, il sofà*
curtain	*la tenda*
carpet	*il tappeto* (rug), *la moquette* (wall-to-wall)
television	*la televisione*
cd player	*il lettore di CD (ci-di)*
lamp	*la lampada*
dvd player	*il DVD (di-vu-di)*
sound system	*lo stereo*
painting/picture	*il quadro*
shelf	*lo scaffale*

stairs	*le scale*
ceiling	*il soffitto*
wall	*il muro, la parete*
floor	*il pavimento*
big/small	*grande/piccolo*
new/old	*nuovo/vecchio*
wood/wooden	*legno, di legno*
plastic/made from plastic	*plastica, di plastica*

B. MORE OR LESS

1. More

più piano	more slowly
più difficile	more difficult
più facile	easier
più lontano	farther
più vicino	nearer
più di quello	more than that
più di un anno	more than a year

2. Less

meno piano	less slowly
meno difficile	less difficult
meno facile	less easy
meno lontano	less far, not so far
meno vicino	less near, not so near
meno di quello	less than that
meno di un anno	less than a year

C. AND, OR, BUT

1. *e* "and"

Roberto e Giovanni sono fratelli.	Robert and John are brothers.

ed can be used instead of *e* before nouns beginning with a vowel:

Roberto ed Andrea sono fratelli.	Robert and Andrew are brothers.

2. *o* "or"

cinque o sei giorni	five or six days
sette o otto ore	seven or eight hours

3. *ma* "but"

Lui non è francese, ma inglese.	He is not French but English.
Lui non viene oggi, ma domani.	He is not coming today but tomorrow.

D. WORD STUDY

catena	chain
lettera	letter
completo	complete
creare	create
eterno	eternal
fontana	fountain
ufficiale	officer

QUIZ 12

1. *inglese*	a. five or six days
2. *e*	b. more than that
3. *ma*	c. seven or eight hours
4. *più facile*	d. English
5. *fratello*	e. but
6. *cinque o sei giorni*	f. tomorrow
7. *meno piano*	g. easier
8. *più di quello*	h. and

9. *domani*   i. less slowly
10. *sette o otto ore*   j. brother

ANSWERS

1—d; 2—h; 3—e; 4—g; 5—j; 6—a; 7—i; 8—b; 9—f;
10—c.

LESSON 13

A. WHERE?

Dove?	Where?
Dov'è?	Where is it?
Dove si trova?	Where is it located (found)?
Qui.	Here.
Lì.	There.
All'angolo.	On the corner.
È in Via Condotti.	It's on the Via Condotti. (*via* = street)
Si trova in Via Condotti.[1]	It's located on the Via Condotti.
È in Piazza Venezia.	It's on Piazza Venezia.
Si trova in Piazza Venezia.	(*piazza* = square)
È in Viale Mazzini.	It's on Viale Mazzini.
Si trova in Viale Mazzini.	(*viale* = avenue)
Per dove? Per quale strada?	Which way?
Per questa strada. Per questa via.	This way.

---

[1] *È* and *si trova* are two interchangeable ways of indicating the location of something.

Per quella strada.	That way.
Come si arriva lì?	How do you get there?
Dov'è questo posto?	Where's that place?
È qui.	It's here.
È proprio qui.	It's right here.
È lì.	It's there.

B. HERE AND THERE

Dov'è il libro?	Where's the book?
È qui.	It's here.
È proprio qui.	It's right here.
È lì.	It's there (where you are).
È la.	It's over there (distant from both of us).
Dov'è Lei?	Where are you?
Sono qui.	Here I am.
Lui è qui.	He is here.
Lui si trova qui.	He's here.
Lui è lì.	He's there.
Eccolo che va via.	There he is, going away.
Eccolo che se ne va.	
È lì, da qualche parte.	It's somewhere over there.
Lo metta qui.	Put it here. *(pol.)*
Lo metta lì.	Put it there. *(pol.)*
Mi aspetti qui.	Wait for me here. *(pol.)*
Mi aspetti lì.	Wait for me there. *(pol.)*
Venga qui.	Come here. *(pol.)*
Eccolo che viene.	Here he comes.
Vada lì.	Go there. *(pol.)*
Fino a lì.	As far as there.
Qui intorno.	Around here.
Qui vicino.	Near here.
Lì in Italia.	Over there in Italy.
Qui in America.	Here in America.

Dove abita lui?	Where does he live?
Lui abita lì.	He lives there.
Io spero di vederlo lì.	I expect to see him there.
Lei è lì.	She's there.
Giovanni abita qui?	Does John live here?
È qui.	It's here. This is the place.
Non è qui.	It's not here.
È lì.	It's there.
Prenda questa strada.	Go this way. (Take this street.) *(pol.)*
Prenda quella strada.	Go that way. (Take that street.) *(pol.)*
Venga per questa strada.	Come this way. (Come by this street.) *(pol.)*
Vada di lì.	Go that way. *(pol.)*
Ho i libri qui.	I have the books here.
Cosa hai lì?	What do you have there?
Sei lì?	Are you there?

C. To the Right, etc.

Dov'è?	Where is it?
A destra.	To the right.
A sinistra.	To the left.
Giri a destra. Svolti a destra.	Turn to your right. *(pol.)*
Giri a sinistra. Svolti a sinistra.	Turn to your left. *(pol.)*
Vada sempre avanti.	Go straight ahead. *(pol.)*
Continui dritto (diritto).	Continue straight ahead. *(pol.)*
È dritto (diritto).	It's straight ahead.
È proprio di fronte.	It's directly opposite.
È sopra.	It's above.
È sotto.	It's below.
È all' angolo.	It's at the corner.

D. Near and Far

qui vicino	near here
molto vicino	very near
a pochi passi da qui	a few steps from here
vicino al paese	near the town
vicino al parco	near the park
vicino alla chiesa	next to the church
È lontano?	Is it far?
È lontano da qui?	Is it far from here?
È più lontano.	It's farther.
È un po' più lontano.	It's a little farther.
Quanto è lontano da qui?	How far is it from here?
È vicino.	It's near.
Non è troppo lontano.	It's not too far.
È lontano da qui?	Is it far from here?
È molto lontano.	It's very far.
Non è molto lontano.	It's not too far.
Si trova a duecento metri da qui.	It's two hundred meters from here.
È a un chilometro da qui.	It's a kilometer from here.

QUIZ 13

1. *lì in Italia*
2. *Mi aspetti qui.*
3. *qui*
4. *a destra*
5. *lì*
6. *È proprio qui.*
7. *Io spero di vederlo lì.*
8. *a sinistra*
9. *È lontano.*
10. *lì dentro*
11. *È lì, da qualche parte.*

a. I expect to see him there.
b. in there
c. to the left
d. It's far.
e. here
f. Wait for me here.
g. straight ahead
h. to the right
i. there
j. Go there.
k. Go that way.

12. *È vicino.*	l. It's right here.
13. *Vada lì.*	m. over there in Italy
14. *Vada per quella strada.*	n. It's somewhere around there.
15. *sempre avanti*	o. It's near.

ANSWERS

1—m; 2—f; 3—e; 4—h; 5—i; 6—l; 7—a; 8—c; 9—d;
10—b; 11—n; 12—o; 13—j; 14—k; 15—g.

REVIEW QUIZ 2

1. _____ (this) *ragazzo*
   a. *questa*
   b. *questo*
   c. *queste*
2. *Dammi* _____ (those, *fem.*).
   a. *quelle*
   b. *queste*
   c. *questo*
3. *Ho* _____ (here) *i libri.*
   a. *lui*
   b. *qui*
   c. *come*
4. *Venga* _____ (here).
   a. *lei*
   b. *lì*
   c. *qui*
5. *Domani vado* _____ (there).
   a. *lì*
   b. *noi*
   c. *come*
6. _____ (Where) *sta?*
   a. *Là*
   b. *Dove*
   c. *Qui*

7. *È* _____ (far) *da qui?*
   a. *lontano*
   b. *quella*
   c. *lì*
8. *Roberto* _____ (and) *Giovanni sono fratelli.*
   a. *con*
   b. *e*
   c. *più*
9. *cinque* _____ (or) *sei giorni*
   a. *o*
   b. *e*
   c. *più*
10. *Desidero venire* _____ (but) *non posso.*
    a. *o*
    b. *ma*
    c. *fino*

ANSWERS

1—b; 2—a; 3—b; 4—c; 5—a; 6—b; 7—a; 8—b; 9—a; 10—b.

LESSON 14

A. I, You, He, ETC. (SUBJECT PRONOUNS)

The use of the subject pronouns is optional: "I speak" is just *parlo;* "we speak," *parliamo;* etc. But the pronouns are used for emphasis or clarity:

Io studio, tu ti diverti.	I study, you enjoy yourself.
Lui è inglese, lei è francese.	He is English; she is French.

SINGULAR

I, You, He, She

io	I
tu	you *(fam.)*
lui	he
lei	she
Lei	you *(pol.)*
io parlo	I speak
tu parli	you speak *(fam.)*
lui parla	he speaks
lei parla	she speaks
Lei parla	you speak *(pol.)*

PLURAL

We, You, They

noi	we
voi	you
loro	they
Loro	you *(formal)*
noi parliamo	we speak
voi parlate	you speak *(plural)*
loro parlano	they speak
Loro parlano	you speak *(formal)*

B.   It's Me (I), You, He, etc.

Sono io.	It's I.
Sei tu.	It's you. *(fam.)*
È lui.	It's he.
È lei.	It's she.
Siamo noi.	It's we.
Siete voi.	It's you. *(plural)*
Sono loro.	It's they.

C. It and Them (Direct Object Pronouns)

	SINGULAR		PLURAL	
MASCULINE	**lo**	it	**li**	them
FEMININE	**la**	it	**le**	them

Ha il denaro?	Do you have the money *(pol.)*
Sì ce l'ho.[1]	Yes I have it.
Ha la borsetta?	Do you have the handbag? *(pol.)*
Sì, ce l'ho.[1]	Yes, I have it.
Ha visto Pietro e Giovanni?	Have you seen Peter and John? *(pol.)*
Sì, (io) li ho visti.	Yes, I have seen them.
Ha visto Maria e Luisa?	Have you seen Mary and Louise? *(pol.)*
Sì, (io) le ho viste.	Yes, I saw them.

Notice that the pronoun agrees in gender and number with the word it refers to. *Lo* and *la* elide; *li* and *le* do not. *Lo* is used when the reference is to an idea or a whole expression:

Lo capisco.	I understand it.

Lo, la, etc. usually come immediately before the verb, as in the case of other object pronouns. However, they may be added to the infinitive (which then drops its final *e):*

Lo voglio capire. = **Voglio capirlo.**	I want to understand it.

D. Word Study

banda	band
composizione	compostion
coscienza	conscience
decorazione	decoration

---

[1] *Lo* and *la* elide to *l'* before vowel sounds.

descrizione	description
missione	mission
numero	number
ottimista	optimist *(masc./fem.)*
regione	region

LESSON 15

A. MY, YOUR, HIS/HER, ETC. (POSSESSIVE ADJECTIVES)

mio, -a, -ei, -e	my
tuo, -a, -oi, -e	your *(fam.)*
suo, -a, -oi, -e	his, her, your *(pol.)*
nostro, -a, -i, -e	our
vostro, -a, -i, -e	your *(pl.)*
loro	their, your *(formal pl.)*

In Italian the possessive adjective is always preceded by the definite article, except when it comes before members of the family in the singular. *Loro* is always preceded by the article.

tuo fratello	your brother
mia figlia	my daughter
il loro figlio	their son

Study the following examples:

SINGULAR

| il mio amico | my friend *(masc.)* |
| la mia amica[1] | my friend *(fem.)* |

[1] Note that the possessive adjective agrees in gender with the noun that follows rather than with the subject: *la mia amica* = my (female) friend. The speaker may be male or female.

il tuo amico	your friend
il suo amico	his/her friend
il nostro amico	our friend
la nostra amica	our friend
il vostro amico	your friend
la vostra amica	your friend
il loro amico	their friend

PLURAL

i miei amici	my friends
i tuoi amici	your friends
i suoi amici	his/her friends
i nostri amici	our friends
le nostre amiche	our friends (fem.)
i vostri amici	your friends
le vostre amiche	your friends (fem.)
i loro amici	their friends

SINGULAR

il mio cappello	my hat
il tuo vestito	your dress/suit
il suo vestito	his/her dress/suit
il nostro amico	our friend
la nostra borsa	our bag
il vostro cavallo	your horse
la vostra penna	your pen

PLURAL

i miei cappelli	my hats
i tuoi vestiti	your clothes
i suoi vestiti	his/her clothes
i nostri amici	our friends
le nostre borse	our bags
i vostri cavalli	your horses
le vostre penne	your pens

B. IT'S MINE, YOURS, HIS, ETC. (POSSESSIVE PRONOUNS)

È mio, mia, etc.[1]	It's mine.
È tuo.	It's yours. *(fam.)*
È Suo.	It's yours. *(pol.)*
È nostro.	It's ours.
È vostro.	It's yours.
È il loro.	It's theirs.
È il mio.	It's mine.
È il tuo.	It's yours.
È il Suo.	It's yours. *(pol.)*
È il nostro.	It's ours.
È il vostro.	It's yours.
È il loro.	It's theirs.

Other examples:

i miei amici ed i tuoi	my friends and yours
Il suo libro è migliore del nostro.	His book is better than ours.

Generally the article is used with the possessive; however, in some cases it is omitted.

Di chi è questa lettera?	Whose is this letter?
È sua.	It's his.

C. TO/FOR/ABOUT ME, YOU, HIM, ETC. (PREPOSITIONAL PRONOUNS)

Notice the form of the pronoun when it comes after a preposition (see Section 32 in the Grammar Summary for more prepositions):

---

[1] As with possessive adjectives, the gender of possessive pronouns depends on the noun they are replacing rather than the gender of the speaker.

per me	for me
per te	for you
con lui	with him
a lei	to her
a te	for you
senza di noi	without us
con voi	with you
per loro	for them
di voi	of, about you

Io parlo di te.	I'm speaking about you.
Marco va senza di noi.	Mark is going without us.
Vuole andare con me.	He wants to go with me.
Lei parla di lui.	She is speaking about him.
Scrivono a voi.	They write to you.

D. DIRECT AND INDIRECT OBJECT PRONOUNS

1. Direct object pronouns take the place of the direct object in a sentence; they receive the action of the verb. In Lesson 14, Section C, *lo/la* and *li/le* (it and them) appeared; the following group of phrases shows all the direct object pronouns:

   a. He sees me, you, him, etc.

Lui mi vede.	He sees me.
Lui ti vede.	He sees you. *(fam.)*
Io lo vedo.	I see him.
Io la vedo.	I see her.
Io La vedo.	I see you. *(pol.)*
Loro ci vedono.	They see us.
Noi vi vediamo.	We see you. *(fam. pl.)*
Noi li vediamo.	We see them. *(masc.)*
Noi le vediamo.	We see them. *(fem.)*

b. She buys it.

Maria lo compra.	Maria buys it. (a *masc. sing.* noun)
Maria la compra.	Maria buys it. (a *fem. sing.* noun)
Maria li compra.	Maria buys them. (a *masc. plur.* noun)
Maria le compra.	Maria buys them. (a *fem. plur.* noun)

2. Indirect object pronouns indicate the person to whom an action occurs, and they are the ultimate recipients of the verb's action. (In English, you sometimes use "to" before the indirect object pronoun.) Study these phrases:

a. He tells me . . .

Lui mi dice . . .	He tells me . . .
Lui ti dice . . .	He tells you . . . *(fam. sing.)*
Lui gli dice . . .	He tells him . . .
Lui le dice . . .	He tells her . . .
Lui ci dice . . .	He tells us . . .
Lui vi dice . . .	He tells you . . .
Lui dice a loro . . .	He tells them . . .

b. I'm speaking to you.

Io Le parlo.	I'm speaking to you. *(pol.)*
Lui ti parla.	He is speaking to you.
Lui Le parla.	He is speaking to you. *(pol.)*

3. When there are two object pronouns in a sentence, the indirect precedes the direct, and both precede the conjugated verb[1]:

[1] See also Section 28 in the Grammar Summary.

a. He gives it to me.

Lui me lo dà.	He gives it to me.
Lui te lo dà.	He gives it to you. *(fam. sing.)*
Lui glielo dà.	He gives it to him/her/you. *(polite)*
Lui ce lo dà.	He gives it to us.
Lui ve lo dà.	He gives it to you.
Lui glielo dà.	He gives it to them.
Lui lo dà a loro.	He gives it to them.

Notice the change in the form of some of the pronouns according to their position in the sentence. Remember that *loro* always follows the verb.

E. MYSELF, YOURSELF, HIMSELF, ETC. (REFLEXIVE PRONOUNS)

1. Notice the forms for "myself," "yourself," etc.: *mi, ti, si,* etc. Verbs that take these "reflexive pronouns" are called "reflexive" verbs.

lavarsi	to wash up, to wash oneself
Io mi lavo.	I wash myself.
Tu ti lavi.	You wash yourself.
Lui si lava.	He washes himself.
Lei si lava.	She washes herself./You wash yourself. *(polite)*
Noi ci laviamo.	We wash ourselves.
Voi vi lavate.	You wash yourselves.
Loro si lavano.	They wash themselves./You wash yourselves. *(formal)*

Other examples:

| Come si chiama? | What's your name? (How do you call yourself?) |

Noi ci vediamo nello specchio.	We see ourselves in the mirror.

2. Many verbs that are reflexive in Italian are not in English:

Mi diverto.	I'm having a good time.
Mi siedo.	I sit down. I'm sitting down.
Mi alzo.	I get up. I'm getting up (standing up).
Mi dimentico.	I forget.
Mi ricordo.	I remember.
Mi fermo.	I stop.
M'addormento.	I fall asleep.
Mi sbaglio.	I'm mistaken.

3. In Italian you don't say "I'm washing my hands," but "I'm washing myself the hands"; not "Take your hat off," but "Take yourself the hat off":

Io mi lavo le mani.	I'm washing my hands.
Si tolga il cappello.	Take your hat off. *(polite)*
Lui si è rotto il braccio.	He broke his arm.
Lei si è tagliata (fem.) il dito.	She cut her finger.
Mi sono fatta (fem.) male alla mano.	I've hurt my hand.

4. The reflexives are also used in the expression *mi fa male* . . . and in the impersonal construction.

Mi fa male la testa. Ho mal di testa.	My head hurts. I have a headache.
Mi fa male lo stomaco. Ho mal di stomaco.	My stomach hurts. I have a stomachache.
Qui si parla italiano.	Italian is spoken here.
Le porte si aprono alle otto.	The doors open at eight.

Si dice che . . .   It's said that . . . People say
that . . . They say that . . .

Qui si mangia bene.   The food's good here. (One
eats well here.)

QUIZ 14

1. *Mi siedo.*
2. *M'addormento.*
3. *Mi diverto.*
4. *Mi ricordo.*
5. *Mi alzo.*
6. *Mi lavo.*
7. *Mi sbaglio.*
8. *Si siedono.*
9. *Mi dimentico.*
10. *Mi fermo.*

a. I get up.
b. I stop.
c. I forget.
d. I'm mistaken.
e. I wash myself.
f. I'm having a good time.
g. They sit down.
h. I remember.
i. I fall asleep.
j. I sit down.

ANSWERS
1—j; 2—i; 3—f; 4—h; 5—a; 6—e; 7—d; 8—g; 9—c;
10—b.

REVIEW QUIZ 3

1. *È* _____ (he).
    a. *lei*
    b. *lui*
    c. *io*
2. *Siamo* _____ (we).
    a. *loro*
    b. *tu*
    c. *noi*
3. *Io do il libro a* _____ (him).
    a. *lui*
    b. *voi*
    c. *loro*

4. *il* _____ (her) *vestito*
    a. *suo*
    b. *mio*
    c. *nostro*

5. *la* _____ (our) *carta*
    a. *nostro*
    b. *nostra*
    c. *tuo*

6. *Dove sono i* _____ (my) *libri?*
    a. *tuoi*
    b. *miei*
    c. *nostri*

7. *Il suo libro è migliore del* _____ (ours).
    a. *tuoi*
    b. *nostro*
    c. *suoi*

8. *Parliamo di* _____ (him).
    a. *te*
    b. *loro*
    c. *lui*

9. *Lui* _____ (to us) *lo dice.*
    a. *lui*
    b. *ce*
    c. *voi*

10. *Come si* _____ (call) *lei?*
    a. *lava*
    b. *chiama*
    c. *vede*

11. *Noi ci* _____ (wash).
    a. *lava*
    b. *lavano*
    c. *laviamo*

12. *Mi* _____ (to be mistaken).
    a. *sbaglio*
    b. *lavo*
    c. *giro*

13. *Mi* _____ (sit down).
    a. *vado*
    b. *ricordo*
    c. *siedo*
14. *Mi sono* _____ (hurt) *alla mano*.
    a. *sbagliato*
    b. *lavo*
    c. *fatto male*
15. *Qui* _____ (is spoken) *italiano*.
    a. *si parla*
    b. *si mangia*
    c. *si chiama*

ANSWERS

1—b; 2—c; 3—a; 4—a; 5—b; 6—b; 7—b; 8—c; 9—b;
10—b; 11—c; 12—a; 13—c; 14—c; 15—a.

SUPPLEMENTAL VOCABULARY 5: THE HUMAN BODY

head	*la testa*
face	*la faccia*
forehead	*la fronte*
eye	*l'occhio*
eyebrow	*il sopracciglio (m.)* *le sopracciglia (f.)*
eyelashes	*il ciglio (m.), le ciglia (f. pl.)*
ear	*l'orecchio (m.),* *le orecchie (f. pl.)*
nose	*il naso*
mouth	*la bocca*
tooth	*il dente*
tongue	*la lingua*
cheek	*la guancia*
chin	*il mento*

hair	*i capelli*
neck	*il collo*
chest	*il petto*
breast	*il seno*
shoulders	*le spalle*
arm	*il braccio (m.), le braccia (f. pl.)*
elbow	*il gomito*
wrist	*il polso*
hand	*la mano le mani*
waist	*la vita*
hips	*i fianchi*
stomach/abdomen	*lo stomaco* (above the waist), *la pancia, il ventre* (below the waist)
penis	*il pene*
vagina	*la vagina*
behind	*il sedere*
leg	*la gamba*
knee	*il ginocchio (m.), le ginocchia (f. pl.)*
ankle	*la caviglia*
foot	*il piede*
finger	*il dito (m.), le dita (f. pl.)*
toe	*l'alluce (m.)*
thumb	*il pollice*
skin	*la pelle*
blood	*il sangue*
brain	*il cervello*
heart	*il cuore*
lungs	*i polmoni*
bone	*l'osso (m.), le ossa (f. pl.)*
muscle	*il muscolo*
tendon	*il tendine*

LESSON 16

A. SOME ACTION PHRASES

Stia attento(-a)! Attenzione!	Watch out! *(pol.)*
Faccia attenzione!	Be careful! Watch out! *(pol.)*
Attento *(-a)*!	
Presto!	Fast! Hurry up!
Vada presto! Corra!	Go fast! Run! *(pol.)*
Più presto!	Faster!
Non tanto di corsa.	Not so fast.
Non molto in fretta.	Not very fast. Not in a hurry.
Non di corsa.	
Più piano. Senza fretta.	Slower. No hurry.
Meno in fretta.	Slower.
Vengo. Io vengo. Sto	I'm coming.
venendo.	
Vengo subito. Corro.	I'm coming right away.
Corra. Faccia presto.	Hurry up. *(pol.)*
Non c'è fretta. Non corra.	There's no hurry. Don't rush (run). *(pol.)*
Io ho fretta.	I'm in a hurry.
Non ho fretta.	I'm not in a hurry.
Un momento!	Just a minute! In a minute!
Al volo. Subito.	Right away.
Immediatamente.	Immediately.
Venga subito! Corra!	Come right away. *(pol.)*
Presto.	Soon.
Immediatamente.	Immediately.
Più presto.	Sooner.
Più tardi.	Later.

B. MAY I ASK ... ?

Posso farLe una domanda?	May I ask you a question?
Posso domandarLe ... ?	May I ask (you) ... ?
Posso chiederLe ... ?	
Puó dirmi ... ?	Can you tell me ... ?
Potrebbe dirmi ... ?	Could you tell me ... ?
Mi vuole dire ... ?	Will you tell me ... ?
Potrebbe dirmi ..., per favore?	Could you please tell me ... ?
Vuole farmi il piacere di dirmi ... ?	Could you please tell me ... ? (formal)
Che cosa vuol dire?	What do you mean?
Io voglio dire che ...	I mean that ...
Che cosa significa questo?	What does this mean?
Questo significa ...	This means ...

C. WORD STUDY

destinazione	destination
diversione	diversion
liquido	liquid
obbligazione	obligation
occupazione	occupation
popolare	popular
solido	solid
teatro	theater

QUIZ 15

1. *Stia attento(-a)!*   a. Will you tell me ... ?
   Attenzione!
2. *Io ho fretta.*   b. Right away.
3. *Io voglio dire che ...*   c. Come right away!
4. *Presto.*   d. I'm coming!

5. *Che cosa significa questo?*	e. Watch out!
6. *Più tardi.*	f. Later.
7. *Mi vuole dire . . . ?*	g. I'm in a hurry.
8. *Vengo! Sto venendo!*	h. I want to say that . . .
9. *Venga subito! Corra!*	i. What does this mean?
10. *Subito.*	j. Soon.

ANSWERS

1—e; 2—g; 3—h; 4—j; 5—i; 6—f; 7—a; 8—d; 9—c;
10—b.

LESSON 17

A. NUMBERS

uno	one
due	two
tre	three
quattro	four
cinque	five
sei	six
sette	seven
otto	eight
nove	nine
dieci	ten
undici	eleven
dodici	twelve
tredici	thirteen
quattordici	fourteen
quindici	fifteen
sedici	sixteen
diciassette	seventeen

diciotto	eighteen
diciannove	nineteen
venti	twenty
ventuno	twenty-one
ventidue	twenty-two
ventitrè	twenty-three
trenta	thirty
trentuno	thirty-one
trentadue	thirty-two
trentatrè	thirty-three
quaranta	forty
quarantuno	forty-one
quarantadue	forty-two
quarantatrè	forty-three
cinquanta	fifty
cinquantuno	fifty-one
cinquantadue	fifty-two
cinquantatrè	fifty-three
sessanta	sixty
sessantuno	sixty-one
sessantadue	sixty-two
sessantatrè	sixty-three
settanta	seventy
settantuno	seventy-one
settantadue	seventy-two
settantatrè	seventy-three
ottanta	eighty
ottantuno	eighty-one
ottantadue	eighty-two
ottantatrè	eighty-three
novanta	ninety
novantuno	ninety-one
novantadue	ninety-two
novantatrè	ninety-three

cento	hundred
centouno	a hundred and one
centodue	a hundred and two
centotrè	a hundred and three
mille	thousand
milledue	a thousand and two
milletrè	a thousand and three

B. More Numbers

centoventi	120
centoventidue	122
centotrenta	130
centoquaranta	140
centocinquanta	150
centosessanta	160
centosettanta	170
centosettantuno	171
centosettantotto	178
centottanta	180
centottantadue	182
centonovanta	190
centonovantotto	198
centonovantanove	199
duecento	200
trecentoventiquattro	324
ottocentosettantacinque	875

primo	*-a, -i, -e*	first
secondo	*-a, -i, -e*	second
terzo	*-a, -i, -e*	third
quarto	*-a, -i, -e*	fourth
quinto	*-a, -i, -e*	fifth
sesto	*-a, -i, -e*	sixth
settimo	*-a, -i, -e*	seventh
ottavo	*-a, -i, -e*	eighth

nono	*-a, -i, -e*	ninth
decimo	*-a, -i, -e*	tenth

due e due fanno quattro	two and two are four
due più due fanno quattro	two and two are four
quattro più due fanno sei	four and two are six
dieci meno due fanno otto	ten minus two is eight

C. WORD STUDY

amministrazione	administration
carattere	character
curioso	curious
tenda	curtain
dizionario	dictionary
grado	degree
ufficiale	official
piatto	plate

QUIZ 16

1. *mille*	a. 1,002
2. *undici*	b. 32
3. *cento*	c. 102
4. *diciassette*	d. 324
5. *trenta*	e. 11
6. *venti*	f. 1,000
7. *sessanta*	g. 60
8. *trecentoventiquattro*	h. 71
9. *trentadue*	i. 17
10. *centodue*	j. 875
11. *ottocentosettantacinque*	k. 83
12. *settantuno*	l. 93
13. *milledue*	m. 20
14. *novantatrè*	n. 30
15. *ottantatrè*	o. 100

LESSON 18

A. How Much?

Quanto costa questo?	How much does this cost?
Costa un euro.	It costs one euro.
Quanto costa un chilo di caffè?	How much is a kilo of coffee?
Costa cinque euro.	It costs five euros.

B. It Costs . . .

Costa . . .	It costs . . .
Questo libro costa dieci euro.	This book costs ten euros.
Lui ha comprato un automobile per quindicimila euro.	He bought a car for fifteen thousand euros.
Il viaggio in treno da Roma a Milano costa cinquantacinque euro.	The trip by train from Rome to Milan costs fifty-five euros.
Ho risparmiato trecento euro per comprarmi un abito.	I've saved three hundred euros to buy a suit.
Lui ha guadagnato nel mese di giugno duemilaottocentotrenta-quattro euro.	He made 2,834 euros in the month of June.
Si vende solamente al chilo e costa un euro e cinquanta.	It's sold only by the kilo and costs one euro fifty (cents).

C. MY ADDRESS IS . . .

Io abito in Via Nazionale, al numero duecento cinquanta.	I live at 250 Nazionale Street.
Lei abita in Corso Italia al numero trecento.	She lives at 300 Corso Italia.
Il negozio si trova in Viale Mazzini, al numero trecentoventisei.	The store is at 326 Mazzini Avenue.
Loro si sono trasferiti in Piazza Venezia, al numero novecento-ventuno.	They moved to 921 Venezia Square.

D. MY TELEPHONE NUMBER IS . . .

Qual'è il suo numero di telefono?	What's your telephone number?
Il mio numero di telefono è sei tre due otto otto tre tre.	My telephone number is 63-28-833.
Il loro numero di telefono è quattro zero otto sei zero due quattro.	Their telephone number is 40-86-024.
Non dimentichi il mio numero di cellulare: otto sei cinque zero sei cinque sette.	Don't forget my telephone number: 86-50-657.
Centralinista, mi dia il numero quattro zero tre sei nove quattro sette.	Operator, may I have 40-36-947?
Il numero quattro zero tre sei nove quattro sette non risponde.	There's no answer at number 40-36-947.

E. THE NUMBER IS . . .

Il numero è . . .	The number is . . .
Il mio numero è . . .	My number is . . .

Il numero della mia camera è trenta.	My room number is 30.
Io sto nella camera numero trenta.	I am in room 30.
Il numero della mia casa è milletrecentoventidue.	My address (house number) is 1322.
Io abito al numero trecento trentadue della Quinta Avenue, al quinto piano.	I live at 332 Fifth Avenue, on the fifth floor.

LESSON 19

A. What's Today?

Che giorno della settimana è oggi?	What day of the week is today?
È lunedì.	It's Monday.
È martedì.	It's Tuesday.
È mercoledì.	It's Wednesday.
È giovedì.	It's Thursday.
È venerdì.	It's Friday.
È sabato.	It's Saturday.
È domenica.	It's Sunday.

To say, "on Sunday . . ." etc. in Italian, simply state the day:

Arrivo sabato.	I arrive (on) Saturday.
Vada lunedì.	Go (on) Monday.

To express a habitual action, use the definite article with the day of the week:

Non lavoriamo il sabato.	We don't work on Saturdays.
Mangio tardi la domenica.	I eat late on Sundays.

The following expressions all mean "What's the date?":

Quanti ne abbiamo?	(How many days do we have?)
Qualè la data di oggi?	(What is the date today?)
Che giorno è oggi?	(What day is today?)

The following expressions all mean "It's the 20th":

È il venti.	(It's the 20th.)
Ne abbiamo venti.	(We have twenty of them.)

On + days of the month is expressed by the masculine definite article + a cardinal number, except for the first of the month, which is *il primo:*

il primo luglio	on July 1
il cinque aprile	on April 5
Che giorno è oggi?	What's today's date?
È il primo maggio.	It's the 1st of May.
È l'undici aprile.	It's the 11th of April.
È il quattro luglio.	It's the 4th of July.
È il quindici settembre.	It's the 15th of September.
È il ventun giugno.	It's the 21st of June.
È il venticinque dicembre.	It's the 25th of December.
È il diciassette novembre.	It's the 17th of November.
È il tredici febbraio.	It's the 13th of February.
È il ventotto agosto.	It's the 28th of August.

B.   SOME DATES

"I Promessi Sposi" fu pubblicato nel milleottocentoventicinque.	"I Promessi Sposi" ("The Betrothed") was published in 1825.
Dante nacque nel milleduecentosessantacinque, e morì nel milletrecentoventuno.	Dante was born in 1265, and died in 1321.
Noi siamo stati lì nel millenovecentottantaquattro.	We were there in 1984.

Oggi è il ventidue febbraio   Today is February 22, 2005.
   duemilacinque.

Il suo compleanno è il   His birthday is January 15.
   quindici gennaio.

Nel diciannovesimo   In the 19th century . . .
   secolo . . .

Negli anni sessanta . . .   In the Sixties . . .

C. Word Study

conclusione	conclusion
cemento	cement
contratto	contract
decisione	decision
persona	person
segnale	signal
stagione	season
stazione	station

QUIZ 17

1. *È lunedì.*
2. *Che giorno è oggi?*
3. *il primo luglio*
4. *Qualè la data di oggi?*
5. *l' undici aprile*
6. *il ventotto febbraio*
7. *il venticinque giugno*
8. *nel millenovecento novanta*
9. *il tredici agosto*
10. *data*

a. the 25th of June
b. the 28th of February
c. the 13th of August
d. in 1990
e. It's Monday.
f. What day is it today?
g. date
h. July first
i. the 11th of April
j. What's today's date?

ANSWERS

1—e; 2—f; 3—h; 4—j; 5—i; 6—b; 7—a; 8—d; 9—c; 10—g.

LESSON 20

A. What Time Is It?

Che ora è?	What time is it?
È l'una.	It's 1:00 o'clock.
Sono le due.	It's 2:00.
Sono le tre.	It's 3:00.
Sono le quattro.	It's 4:00.
Sono le cinque.	It's 5:00.
Sono le sei.	It's 6:00.
Sono le sette.	It's 7:00.
Sono le otto.	It's 8:00.
Sono le nove.	It's 9:00.
Sono le dieci.	It's 10:00.
Sono le undici.	It's 11:00.
Sono le dodici.	It's 12:00 noon.
È mezzogiorno.	It's noon.
È mezzanotte.	It's midnight.
minuto	minute
ora	hour
Che ora è, per favore?	What time is it, please?
Ha l'ora, per favore?	Do you have the time, please?
Il mio orologio fa le cinque.	It's 5 o'clock by my watch. (My watch marks 5 o'clock.)
È l'una e cinque.	It's 1:05.
È l'una e dieci.	It's 1:10.
È l'una e quindici.	It's 1:15.
È l'una e un quarto.	It's 1:15.
È l'una e mezza.	It's 1:30.
È l'una e cinquanta.	It's 1:50.
Sono le due meno dieci.	It's 1:50. (two less ten)
Sono le tre e dieci.	It's 3:10. (three and ten)
Sono le sei e tre quarti.	It's 6:45. (six and three quarters)

Sono le due meno un quarto.	It's 1:45. (two less a quarter)
Non sono ancora le quattro.	It's not four yet.
A che ora parte il treno?	At what time does the train leave?
Alle nove in punto.	At 9 o'clock sharp.
Alle nove precise.	Exactly at 9 o'clock.
Alle nove circa.	About 9 o'clock.
Verso le nove.	Around 9 o'clock.

B. AT WHAT TIME?

A che ora?	At what time?
All'una.	At one o'clock.
Alle sette di mattina.	At 7 A.M.
Alle tre meno venti del pomeriggio.	At 2:40 P.M. (three minus twenty in the afternoon)
Alle quindici meno venti.	At 14:40 P.M. (fifteen hours less twenty minutes)
Alle sei di sera.	At 6 P.M.
Alle diciotto.	At 18:00.
Alle sei del pomeriggio.	At 6 P.M.

Notice that when you want to specify "A.M." or "P.M." in Italian, you add *di mattina* (in the morning), *del pomeriggio* (in the afternoon), *di sera* (in the evening), *di notte* (at night). In Italy, as in most European countries, the 24-hour clock (used by the military in the U.S.) is generally used for transportation schedules and theater times. From 1 A.M. to 12:00 noon, the time is the same as the 12-hour system. After noon, just keep counting, so that 1 P.M. is 13 hours, 2 P.M. is 14 hours, etc. Midnight, or 24 hours, is also expressed as 00:00.

C. It's Time

È ora.	It's time.
È ora di farlo.	It's time to do it.
È ora di partire.	It's time to leave.
È ora di andare a casa.	It's time to go home.
Ho molto tempo.	I have a lot of time.
Non ho tempo.	I don't have any time.
Lui sta perdendo tempo.	He is wasting (losing)
Perde tempo.	time.
Lui viene di tanto in tanto.	He comes from time to time.

D. Word Study

assoluto	absolute
aspetto	aspect
bar	bar
cambio	exchange
certo	certain
combinazione	combination
maniera	manner
pericolo	danger
rischio	risk

QUIZ 18

1. *È ora di farlo.*	a. He comes from time to time.
2. *Che ora è?*	b. It's 9:00.
3. *È l'una.*	c. At what time?
4. *Sono le tre.*	d. It's time to do it.
5. *Sono le nove.*	e. It's 2:00.
6. *È mezzanotte.*	f. It's 1:00.
7. *A che ora?*	g. I don't have any time.
8. *Non ho tempo.*	h. It's 2:40 P.M.
9. *È l'una e un quarto.*	i. It's noon.

10. *Sono le quattro.*	j. It's 3:00.
11. *Sono le due.*	k. It's 1:05.
12. *Lui viene di tanto in tanto.*	l. It's 4:00.
13. *È mezzogiorno.*	m. What time is it?
14. *È l'una e cinque.*	n. It's 1:15.
15. *Sono le tre meno venti del pomeriggio.*	o. It's midnight.

ANSWERS

1—d; 2—m; 3—f; 4—j; 5—b; 6—o; 7—c; 8—g; 9—n;
10—l; 11—e; 12—a; 13—i; 14—k; 15—h.

LESSON 21

A.   YESTERDAY, TODAY, TOMORROW, ETC.

PASSATO	PRESENTE	FUTURO
ieri	**oggi**	**domani**
yesterday	today	tomorrow
ieri mattina	**stamattina**	**domani mattina**
yesterday morning	**(questa mattina)** this morning	**(domattina)** tomorrow morning
ieri sera	**stasera**	**domani sera**
last evening	**(questa sera)** this evening	tomorrow evening
ieri notte	**questa notte**	**domani notte**
last night	**(stanotte)** tonight	tomorrow night

B. MORNING, NOON, NIGHT, ETC.

stamattina (questa mattina)	this morning
ieri mattina	yesterday morning
domani mattina	tomorrow morning
questo pomeriggio	this afternoon
ieri pomeriggio	yesterday afternoon
domani pomeriggio	tomorrow afternoon
stasera (questa sera)	this evening/tonight
ieri sera	yesterday evening/last night
domani sera	tomorrow evening
questa notte (stanotte)	tonight
ieri notte	last night/late after midnight
domani notte	tomorrow night

C. THIS WEEK, NEXT MONTH, IN A LITTLE WHILE, ETC.

questa settimana	this week
la settimana scorsa	last week
la settimana entrante	next week
la settimana prossima	next week
fra due settimane	in two weeks
due settimane fa	two weeks ago
questo mese	this month
il mese scorso	last month
il mese entrante	next month
il mese che viene	the coming month
fra due mesi	in two months
due mesi fa	two months ago
quest'anno	this year
l'anno scorso	last year
l'anno prossimo	next year
l'anno che viene	the coming year

fra due anni	in two years
due anni fa	two years ago
Quanto tempo fa?	How long ago?
un momento fa	a moment ago
molto tempo fa	a long time ago
ora	now, for the time being
in questo momento preciso	at this very moment
da un momento all'altro	at any moment
per il momento	for the time being
in questo momento	at this moment
in breve tempo/*fra poco*	in a short (amount of) time/soon
in poco tempo/*fra poco*	in a short (amount of) time/soon
di tanto in tanto	from time to time
Quante volte?	How many times?
una volta	once
ogni volta	each time
due volte	twice
raramente	rarely
non spesso	not often
molte volte	many times, often
molto spesso	very often
a volte/qualche volta	sometimes
ogni tanto	once in a while
di tanto in tanto	now and then; from time to time
di mattina presto	early in the morning
la sera/al crepuscolo	in the evening/at twilight
al tramonto	at nightfall
il giorno seguente	the following day
il giorno dopo	the day after
fra due settimane	in two weeks
fra una settimana	in a week
domani alle otto	tomorrow at eight
mercoledì prossimo	next Wednesday

il lunedì della settimana scorsa/lunedì scorso	Monday of last week/last Monday
il cinque di questo mese	the fifth of this month
il cinque del mese passato	the fifth of last month
all'inizio di marzo	at the beginning of March
alla fine del mese	at the end of the month
all'inizio dell'anno	in the early part of the year
verso la fine dell'anno	toward the end of the year
Avvenne otto anni fa.	It happened eight years ago.
È successo otto anni fa.	It happened eight years ago.

QUIZ 19

1. *ieri mattina*	a. last year
2. *questa sera*	b. last night
3. *domani sera*	c. today at noon
4. *ieri sera*	d. now
5. *il mese entrante*	e. in two weeks
6. *ora*	f. in a little while/soon
7. *la settimana scorsa*	g. yesterday morning
8. *l'anno scorso*	h. from time to time
9. *oggi a mezzogiorno*	i. It happened eight years ago.
10. *fra poco*	j. this evening
11. *questa settimana*	k. sometimes
12. *Avvenne otto anni fa.*	l. in a week
13. *verso la fine dell'anno*	m. tomorrow evening
14. *due mesi fa*	n. next month
15. *verso la fine del mese*	o. last week
16. *fra una settimana*	p. each time
17. *di tanto in tanto*	q. about the end of the month
18. *a volte*	r. toward the end of the year
19. *fra due settimane*	s. this week
20. *ogni volta*	t. two months ago

1—g; 2—j; 3—m; 4—b; 5—n; 6—d; 7—o; 8—a; 9—c;
10—f; 11—s; 12—i; 13—r; 14—t; 15—q; 16—l; 17—h;
18—k; 19—e; 20—p.

REVIEW QUIZ 4

1. *Compro un' automobile per* _____ (thirty thousand)
   euro.
   a. *tremila*
   b. *quattrocento*
   c. *trentamila*
2. *Il suo numero di telefono è* _____ (408-60-42).
   a. *sei, cinque, zero, sei, nove, sei, zero*
   b. *tre, sei, nove, due, zero, quattro, due*
   c. *quattro, zero, otto, sei, zero, quattro, due*
3. *Qualè la* _____ (date) *di oggi?*
   a. *giorno*
   b. *mese*
   c. *data*
4. *Che* _____ (day) *è oggi?*
   a. *mese*
   b. *giorno*
   c. *come*
5. *il* _____ (17) *dicembre*
   a. *diciassette*
   b. *ventisette*
   c. *cinque*
6. *È* _____ (1:10).
   a. *l' una e cinque*
   b. *l' una e dieci*
   c. *l' una e un quarto*
7. *Sono le* _____ (7).
   a. *sette*
   b. *nove*
   c. *sei*

8. *È* _____ (12 noon).
   a. *mezzanotte*
   b. *mezzogiorno*
   c. *undici*

9. *Sono le* _____ (2:40).
   a. *le quattro meno un quarto*
   b. *le tre meno venti*
   c. *le due meno un quarto*

10. _____ (yesterday) *mattina*
    a. *oggi*
    b. *ieri*
    c. *e*

11. *la* _____ (week) *scorsa*
    a. *settimana*
    b. *notte*
    c. *domani*

12. *fra due* _____ (months)
    a. *settimane*
    b. *giorni*
    c. *mesi*

13. *Sono due* _____ (years).
    a. *mesi*
    b. *anni*
    c. *giorni*

14. *il* _____ (Wednesday) *prossimo*
    a. *lunedì*
    b. *venerdì*
    c. *mercoledì*

15. *alla* _____ (end) *dell'anno*
    a. *fine*
    b. *inizio*
    c. *primo*

ANSWERS

1—c; 2—c; 3—c; 4—b; 5—a; 6—b; 7—a; 8—b; 9—b;
10—b; 11—a; 12—c; 13—b; 14—c; 15—a.

LESSON 22

A. NOT, NOTHING, NEVER, NO ONE

The word for "not," *non,* comes before the verb:

io non vedo	I don't see
tu non vedi	you don't see
Non vedo nulla.	I see nothing. I don't see anything.
Non vado mai.	I never go.
Non vengono.	They are not coming.
Non vedo niente.	I see nothing. I don't see anything.
Non vado mai via.	I never go away.
Nessuno viene.	No one is coming.
Non viene nessuno.	
Sì, signore.	Yes, sir.
No, signora.	No, ma'am.
Dice di sì.	He (She) says yes.
Dice di no.	He (She) says no.
Credo di sì.	I think so.
Non è bene.	It's not good.
Non è male.	It's not bad.
Non è quello.	It's not that.
Non è qui.	He's (She's) not here.
Non è troppo.	It's not too much.
Non è abbastanza.	It's not enough.
È abbastanza.	It's enough.
Non tanto in fretta.	Not so fast.
Non così in fretta.	
Non tanto spesso.	Not so often.
Non così spesso.	
Non è nulla. È nulla.	It's nothing.
Questo è nulla. Ciò è nulla.	That's nothing.
Non è molto importante.	It's not very important.

Non ho tempo.	I have no time.
Non so nè come nè quando.	I don't know how or when.
Non so dove.	I don't know where.
Non so nulla.	I don't know anything.
Non so niente.	
Non ne so nulla.	I know nothing about it.
Non so nulla di ciò.	
Non voglio nulla.	I don't want anything.
Non desidero nulla.	
Non importa.	It doesn't matter. It's not
Non fa niente.	important.
Non me ne importa.	I don't care. It makes no difference to me.
Non me ne importa niente.	I don't care at all.
Non me ne importa affatto.	It doesn't make the slightest difference to me.
Non lo dica.	Don't say it. *(pol.)*
Non ho nulla da dire.	I have nothing to say.
Non lo dirò mai.	I'll never say it.
Non è successo nulla.	Nothing happened.
Non ho niente da fare.	I have nothing to do.
Non lo vedo mai.	I never see him.
Non l'ho mai visto prima.	I've never seen him before.
Non l'ho mai visto.	I've never seen him.
Non viene mai.	He (She) never comes.
Non è mai venuto.	He has never come.
Non vado mai.	I never go.
Non andrò mai.	I'll never go.

B. NEITHER . . . NOR . . .

Non ho detto una parola, nè una sillaba.
I haven't said a word, nor a syllable.

Non posso andare nè voglio andare.
I can't go, nor do I want to go.

Nè ... nè ...
Neither ... nor ...

Nè più nè meno.
Just so (neither more nor less).

Nè l'uno nè l'altro.
Neither the one nor the other. (Neither one.)

Nè questo nè quello.
Neither this nor that.

Nè molto nè poco.
Neither (too) much nor (too) little.

Nè bene nè male.
So-so. Neither good nor bad.

Non ho nè tempo nè denaro.
I have neither the time nor the money.

Non sa nè leggere nè scrivere.
He (She) can neither read nor write.

Non ho nè sigarette nè fiammiferi.
I have neither cigarettes nor matches.

C. WORD STUDY

antagonista	antagonist/opponent
avanzamento	advance
banco	bank
capitolo	chapter
contento	content

delizioso	delicious
energia	energy
errore	mistake
frutto	fruit
ricco	rich

QUIZ 20

1. *Non vedo.*	a. Neither this nor that.
2. *Non è nulla.*	b. I have no time.
3. *Non lo dirò mai.*	c. Don't tell it to me.
4. *Non vado mai via.*	d. Nothing happened.
5. *Lui non vede Giovanni.*	e. I don't see.
6. *Non credo.*	f. I don't know anything.
7. *Non tanto in fretta.*	g. I've never seen him.
8. *Non so nulla.*	h. He doesn't see John.
9. *Non vedo nulla.*	i. I'll never say it.
10. *Io non l' ho mai visto.*	j. He never comes.
11. *Non me ne importa.*	k. I see nothing.
12. *Non è successo nulla.*	l. I'll never go.
13. *Lui non viene mai.*	m. It's nothing.
14. *Non è male.*	n. He's (She's) not here.
15. *Non andrò mai.*	o. I don't think so.
16. *Non è qui.*	p. It's not bad.
17. *Nessuno viene.*	q. I don't care.
18. *Nè questo nè quello.*	r. Not so fast.
19. *Non me lo dica.*	s. I never go away.
20. *Non ho tempo.*	t. No one is coming.

ANSWERS

1—e; 2—m; 3—i; 4—s; 5—h; 6—o; 7—r; 8—f; 9—k;
10—g; 11—q; 12—d; 13—j; 14—p; 15—l; 16—n; 17—t;
18—a; 19—c; 20—b.

LESSON 23

A. ISN'T IT? AREN'T THEY? DON'T YOU?

È vero?
Is it? (Is it true?)

Non è vero?
Isn't it? (Isn't it true?)

L'italiano è facile, non è vero?
Italian is easy, isn't it?

La gente qui è molto gentile, vero?
The people here are very nice, aren't they?

Lei non ha una matita, vero?
You don't have a pencil, do you?

Lei conosce questo posto, non è vero?
You know this place, don't you?

Lei conosce il signor Rossi, vero?
You know Mr. Rossi, don't you?

Lei ha un cucchiaio e un tovagliolo, vero?
You have a spoon and a napkin, don't you?

Lei non è qui da molto tempo, vero?
You haven't been here very long, have you?

Lei verrà, vero?
You will come, won't you?

Fa freddo, vero?
It's cold, isn't it?

È molto carino! Non è carino?
It's very cute! It's cute, isn't it?

Va bene, vero?
It's all right, isn't it?

B. SOME, ANY, A FEW

Ha dei soldi *(Lei)*?
Do you have any money?

Sì, ne ho.
Yes, I have some.

No, non ne ho.
No, I don't have any.

Ha dei soldi *(lui)*?
Does he have any money?

Ne ha.
He has some.

Non ne ha affatto.
He doesn't have any at all.

Ha ancora dei soldi? Le sono rimasti dei soldi?
Do you still have money? Do you have any money left?

Me ne sono rimasti un po'.
I have some left. (Some remains to me.)

Quanti libri ha?
How many books do you have?

Ne ho pochi.
I have few.

Desidera un po' di frutta?
Do you want some fruit?

Me ne dia un po'.
Give me some. *(pol.)*

Ce ne dia un po'.
Give us some. *(pol.)*

Ne dia un po' a lui.
Give him some. *(pol.)*

alcuni dei miei amici
some of my friends

C. LIKE, AS, HOW

come
like, as, how

come me
like me

come quello
like that

come questo
like this

come noi
like us

come gli altri
like the others

Questo non è come quello.
This one isn't like that one.

Come desidera.
As you wish. *(pol.)*

È come a casa propria.
It's like (being at) home.

Lui non è come suo padre.
He's not like his father.

Com' è?
What's it like?

È bianco come la neve.
It's as white as snow.

Come piove!
What rain! (How it's raining!)

Come? Cosa dice?
What? What did you say? What do you mean?

Perchè no? Come no?
Why not?

QUIZ 21

1. *Come desidera.*
2. *come gli altri*
3. *come questo*

a. He's not like his father.
b. What? What did you say?
c. Give him some. *(pol.)*

4. *Ha del denaro (Lei)?*   d. Why not?
5. *alcuni dei miei amici*   e. It's all right, isn't it?
6. *Non è come suo padre.*   f. As you wish. *(pol.)*
7. *Come?*   g. Do you have any money?
8. *Ne dia un po' a lui.*   h. like the others
9. *Perchè no?*   i. like this
10. *Va bene, non è vero?*   j. some of my friends

ANSWERS

1—f; 2—h; 3—i; 4—g; 5—j; 6—a; 7—b; 8—c; 9—d;
10—e.

LESSON 24

A. HAVE YOU TWO MET?

Buon dì. (old fashioned)
Hello.

Salve.
Hi. *(fam.)*

Conosce il mio amico?
Do you know my friend? *(pol.)*

(È un) piacere.
(It's) a pleasure.

Credo che ci siamo già conosciuti.
I believe we've met before.

Non credo di aver avuto il piacere.
I don't believe I've had the pleasure.

Non ho avuto il piacere (di conoscerLa).
I haven't had the pleasure (of meeting you).

Credo che vi conosciate già, non è vero?
I believe you already know each other, don't you?

Credo che ci conosciamo.
I think we know each other.

Ho già avuto il piacere di conoscerlo.
I've already had the pleasure of meeting him.

Mi permetta di presentarLa al mio amico Antonio Marchi.
Allow me to introduce you to my friend Antonio Marchi.

B. HELLO, HOW ARE YOU?

Buon giorno.
Good morning. Good day.

Come sta?
How do you do? How are you? *(pol.)*

Ciao.
Hi. Bye. *(fam.)*

Come stai?
How are you? *(fam.)*

Non c'è male. E Lei?
So-so. And you?

E tu?
And you?

E come sta Lei?
And how are you?

E come stai tu?
And how are you?

Che c'è di nuovo?
What's new?

Niente di nuovo.
Nothing much. (Nothing new.)

Nulla di importante.
Nothing much. (Nothing important.)

C'è niente di nuovo?
(Isn't there) anything new?

Non c'è niente di nuovo.
There's nothing new.

Com'è che non ci si vede mai?
Where have you been? *(fam.)*

Com'è che non La si vede mai?
Where have you been? (How is it that no one ever sees you?)
(pol.)

Sono stato molto occupato(-a) in questi giorni.
I've been very busy these days.

Mi telefoni qualche volta.
Give me a call sometime. *(pol.)*

Le telefonerò uno di questi giorni.
I'll call you one of these days. *(pol.)*

Ti telefonerò uno di questi giorni.
I'll call you one of these days. *(fam.)*

Perchè non viene a trovarci a casa?
Why don't you come to see us (to our house)? *(pol.)*

Verrò a trovarvi la settimana prossima.
I'll come to visit you next week.

Non dimentichi la Sua promessa.
Don't forget your promise. *(pol.)*

Non dimenticare la tua promessa.
Don't forget your promise. *(fam.)*

Alla prossima settimana, allora.
Until next week, then.

Arrivederci alla settimana prossima.
See you next week. (Until next week.)

C. WORD STUDY

angolo	angle
causa	cause
distanza	distance
effetto	effect
industria	industry
opinione	opinion
oscuro	obscure
proprietario	proprietor

LESSON 25

A. GLAD TO HAVE MET YOU

Sono lieto(-*a*) di averLa conosciuta.
Glad to have met you.

Molto lieto(-a).
Glad (happy) to have met you.

Spero di vederLa presto.
Hope to see you again soon.

Lo spero anch'io.
I hope so, too.

Ecco il mio indirizzo e il mio numero di telefono.
Here's my address and telephone number.

Ha il mio indirizzo?
Do you have my address? *(pol.)*

No, me lo dia.
No, let me have it. *(pol.)*

Eccolo qui.
Here it is.

Molte grazie.
Thanks a lot.

Si fa tardi.
It's getting late.

È ora di rientrare.
It's time to go back.

Partiamo domani.
We're leaving tomorrow.

Quando posso telefonarLe?
When can I call you *(pol.)*?

Di mattina.
In the morning.

La chiamerò dopodomani.
I'll call you *(pol.)* the day after tomorrow.

Aspetterò la Sua chiamata.
I'll be expecting your *(pol.)* call.

B. GOOD-BYE

ArrivederLa.
Good-bye. *(pol.).*

Arrivederci.
Good-bye. *(fam.)*

Ciao.
Bye. *(fam.)*

A più tardi.
See you later.

A dopo.
See you later. *(fam.)*

Alla prossima.
Until next time.

A domani.
See you tomorrow. ('till tomorrow.)

A sabato.
See you Saturday. ('till Saturday.)

QUIZ 22

1. *Spero di vederLa presto.*
2. *ArrivederLa.*
3. *Sono lieto(-a) di averLa conosciuta.*
4. *Ha il mio indirizzo?*
5. *Eccolo qui.*
6. *Di mattina.*
7. *A domani.*
8. *Aspetterò la Sua chiamata.*
9. *Molte grazie.*
10. *A sabato.*

a. Do you have my address?
b. See you tomorrow.
c. I'll be expecting your call.
d. 'till Saturday.
e. In the morning.
f. Glad to have met you.
g. Thanks a lot.
h. Hope to see you soon.
i. Here it is.
j. Good-bye.

ANSWERS

1—h; 2—j; 3—f; 4—a; 5—i; 6—e; 7—b; 8—c; 9—g; 10—d.

C. Visiting Someone

Abita qui il signor Giovanni Rossi?
Does Mr. John Rossi live here?

Sì, abita qui.
Yes, he does. (He lives here.)

A che piano?
On what floor?

Terzo piano, a sinistra.
Third floor, on the left.

È in casa il signor Rossi?
Is Mr. Rossi at home?

No, signore. È uscito.
No, sir. He's gone out.

A che ora sarà di ritorno?
A che ora ritornerà?
At what time will he be back?

Non so dirLe.
I couldn't say. (I don't know how to tell you.)

Desidera lasciar detto qualche cosa?
Do you want to leave him a message?

Gli lascerò un biglietto . . .
I'll leave him a note . . .

Se mi può dare una matita e un foglio di carta.
If you can, give me a pencil and a piece of paper.

Ritornerò questa sera.
I'll come back tonight.

Ritornerò domani.
I'll come back tomorrow.

Ritornerò un altro giorno.
I'll come back another day.

Gli dica di telefonarmi, per favore.
Please tell him to call me.

Sarò in casa tutto il giorno.
I'll be at home all day.

QUIZ 23

1. *terzo piano, a sinistra*	a. I'll be at home all day.
2. *Ritornerò più tardi.*	b. Is he at home?
3. *Abita qui il signor Giovanni Rossi?*	c. At what time will he be back?
4. *È uscito.*	d. He lives here.
5. *A che ora ritornerà?*	e. What floor?
6. *È in casa?*	f. Tell him to call me.
7. *Che piano?*	g. He's gone out.
8. *Gli dica di telefonarmi.*	h. Does Mr. John Rossi live here?
9. *Sarò in casa tutto il giorno.*	i. third floor, on the left
10. *Abita qui.*	j. I'll come back later.

ANSWERS

1—i; 2—j; 3—h; 4—g; 5—c; 6—b; 7—e; 8—f; 9—a;
10—d.

LESSON 26

A. PLEASE

The most common ways of saying "please" are *per favore,
per piacere,* or *mi faccia il favore di . . .,* which means literally "would you do me the favor of . . .," and is reserved for
formal settings or written correspondence.

Porti questo, per piacere.
Please carry this.

Entrino, per favore.
Please come in. (speaking to several people)

Per piacere, venga qui.
Please come here.

Per favore, mi faccia vedere i suoi documenti.
Please let me see your papers.

Per piacere, vuole chiamare un tassì?
Per piacere, vuole chiamare un taxi?
Will you please call a taxi?

Mi faccia il favore di venire.
Please come. (Do me the favor of coming.)

B. OTHER POLITE EXPRESSIONS

1. **Mi scusi. Mi perdoni.**
   Excuse me. Pardon me.
   Scusi il ritardo.
   Excuse my lateness.

2. **Per cortesia.**
   Please.
   Per cortesia, il Suo biglietto.
   Your ticket, please.
   Per cortesia, sieda qui.
   Please sit here.

3. **La prego.**
   Please.
   La prego di farlo al più presto possibile.
   Please do it as soon as possible.
   La prego, puo dirmi dov'è la biblioteca?
   Can you please tell me where the library is?

4. **Mi dispiace. Mi spiace. Mi scusi.** (*pol.*)
   I'm sorry.
   Scusami. (*fam.*) **Chiedo scusa.**
   I apologize.

Perdonami, per favore. (per piacere, per cortesia)
Please forgive me.

5. *Desidero,* or *desidererei,* means "I would like to."

Desidera sedersi qui?   Would you like to sit here?
Desidererei andare ma   I'd like to go, but I can't.
  non posso.

C. WORD STUDY

ambizione	ambition
brillante	brilliant
capitale	capital
contratto	contract
democrazia	democracy
dipartimento	department
monumento	monument
ostacolo	obstacle
recente	recent

QUIZ 24

1. *Desidera sedersi qui?*   a. Excuse my lateness.
2. *Per favore, venga qui.*   b. Excuse me. Pardon me.
3. *Per favore, vuole*   c. Please come here.
   chiamare un tassì?
4. *Mi scusi il ritardo.*   d. Please carry this.
5. *Mi scusi. Mi perdoni.*   e. Please tell me where the
                                   library is.
6. *Per favore, entrino.*   f. Your ticket, please.
7. *Per favore, può dirmi*   g. Will you please call a
   dov'è la stazione?   taxi?
8. *Per piacere, porti questo.* h. Please come in.
9. *Per favore, il Suo*   i. Can you please tell me
   biglietto.   where the station is?

10. *Per favore, mi dica*   j. Would you like to sit
    dov' è la biblioteca.   here?

ANSWERS

1—j; 2—c; 3—g; 4—a; 5—b; 6—h; 7—i; 8—d; 9—f; 10—e.

REVIEW QUIZ 5

1. *È in* _____ (home, house) *il signor Rossi?*
   a. *appartamento*
   b. *ora*
   c. *casa*
2. *Desidera lasciare una* _____ (note)?
   a. *matita*
   b. *nota*
   c. *carta*
3. *Mi* _____ (excuse) *il rítardo.*
   a. *la prego*
   b. *scusi*
   c. *faccia*
4. _____ (Hope to) *vederLa presto.*
   a. *Desidero*
   b. *Spero di*
   c. *Sarò*
5. _____ (Please) *lo faccia al più presto possibile.*
   a. *Servire*
   b. *Mi scusi*
   c. *Per piacere*
6. *Ha la faccia bianca* _____ (as) *la neve.*
   a. *cui*
   b. *come*
   c. *questo*
7. _____ (I would like), *ma non posso.*
   a. *Io vorrei*
   b. *Ho*
   c. *Desidera*

8. _____ (Why) *non lo ha detto?*
    a. *Chi*
    b. *Perchè*
    c. *Di chi*

ANSWERS

1—c; 2—b; 3—b; 4—b; 5—c; 6—b; 7—a; 8—b.

LESSON 27

A. WHO? WHAT? WHEN? ETC.

1. *Chi?* = Who?

Chi è?	Who is he (she)?
Non so chi è.	I don't know who he (she) is.
Chi sono?	Who are they?
Chi lo ha detto?	Who said it?
Chi l' ha detto?	Who said so?
Chi l' ha fatto?	Who did it?
Di chi è questa matita?	Whose pencil is this?
Per chi è questo?	Who is this for?
Chi desidera vedere?	Whom do you wish to see?
A chi desidera parlare?	To whom do you wish to speak?
Chi lo sa?	Who knows (it)?
Di chi è questo?	Whose is this?

2. *Che? Che cosa?* = What?

Che cosa è questo?	What's this?
Che cosa è quello?	What's that?
Che cosa succede?	What's the matter? What's up?
Che c'è?	What's the matter? What's up?

Che è successo?	What happened?
Che c'è di nuovo?	What's new?
Cosa pensa? Che cosa pensa?	What do you think?
Cosa sono?	What are they?
Che cosa ha?	What do you have?
Cosa Le succede?	What's the matter with you?
Che ora è?	What time is it?
Che cosa dice?	What are you saying?
Che cosa ha detto?	What did you say?
Di che cosa sta parlando?	What are you talking about?
Di che si tratta?	What is it about?
Che cosa vuole?	What do you want?
Cosa posso fare per Lei?	What can I do for you?
Desidera?	What would you like?
I signori desiderano?	What would you like? *(pol. pl.)*

3. *Perchè?* = Why?

Perchè così?	Why so?
Perchè no?	Why not?
Perchè dice questo?	Why do you say that?
Perchè tanta fretta?	Why are you in such a hurry? Why the hurry?
Perchè l'ha fatto?	Why did you do it? *(pol.)*
Perchè non viene?	Why don't you come?

4. *Come?* = How?

Come si dice questo in italiano?	How do you say this in Italian?
Come si chiama?	What is your name? (How do you call yourself?) *(pol.)*
Come ti chiami?	What is your name? *(fam.)*
Come si scrive questo?	How is this spelled (written)?

5. *Quanto?* = How much?

Quanto denaro desidera?	How much money do you want?
Quanti libri ci sono?	How many books are there?
Quanto è distante Napoli da Firenze?	How far is it from Naples to Florence?

6. *Quale?* = What? Which?

Qualè il suo nome?	What is his name?
Quale desidera?	Which (one) do you want?
Quale desidera, questo o quello?	Which (one) do you want, this one or that one?
Quale di queste matite è la Sua?	Which one of these pencils is yours?
Quale di queste due strade porta a Siena?	Which of these two roads leads to Siena?
Qualè il suo indirizzo?	What's his address?

7. *Dove?* = Where?

Dov'è il Suo amico?	Where is your friend?
Dove vive (lui)?	Where does he live?
Dove va (lei)?	Where is she going?

8. *Quando?* = When?

Quando verrà Suo fratello?	When will your brother come?
Quando è successo?	When did it happen?
Quando parte?	When are you going (leaving)?
Non so quando.	I don't know when.
Fino a quando?	Until when?
Per quanto tempo?	For how long?
Non so fino a quando.	I don't know how long. (I don't know until when.)

Quando? Fra quanto tempo?	When?
Quando Lei vuole.	When you wish.
Da quando?	Since when?
Com'è avvenuto?	How did it happen?
Quando è accaduto?	When did it happen?
Da quando è qui?	How long have you been here? *(pol.)*

QUIZ 25

1. *Come si chiama?*	a. When did it happen?
2. *Quanti libri ci sono?*	b. Since when?
3. *Come si dice questo in italiano?*	c. Who knows?
4. *Che cosa dice?*	d. Where does he live?
5. *Quando è successo?*	e. What's your name?
6. *Da quando?*	f. What are you saying?
7. *Chi lo sa?*	g. Why not?
8. *Perchè no?*	h. How do you write this?
9. *Dove abita (lui)?*	i. How many books are there?
10. *Come si scrive questo?*	j. How do you say this in Italian?

ANSWERS

1—e; 2—i; 3—j; 4—f; 5—a; 6—b; 7—c; 8—g; 9—d; 10—h.

B. WHAT A PITY! WHAT A SURPRISE!

Che peccato!	What a pity!
Che vergogna!	What a shame!
Che disgrazia!	How unfortunate! (What a misfortune!)
Che orrore!	How awful!

Che fortuna!   What luck! How lucky!
Che sorpresa!   What a surprise!
Com'è carino!   How cute (he/it is)!
Com'è grazioso! Com'è How beautiful!
  bello!

REVIEW QUIZ 6

1. *Non vedo* _____ (nothing).
   a. *nessuno*
   b. *nulla*
   c. *mai*
2. *Non viene* _____ (nobody).
   a. *nessuno*
   b. *no*
   c. *mai*
3. *Non sa leggere* _____ (nor) *scrivere*.
   a. *no*
   b. *mai*
   c. *nè*
4. *L'italiano è facile,* _____ (isn't it)?
   a. *non è vero*
   b. *è vero*
   c. *no*
5. *Me ne dia* _____ (a little).
   a. *nulla*
   b. *un po'*
   c. *qualcosa*
6. *Desidera* _____ (some) *di frutta?*
   a. *alcuni*
   b. *pochi*
   c. *un po'*
7. *Non è* _____ (like) *suo padre*.
   a. *come*
   b. *è*
   c. *li altri*

8. *È stato molto* _____ (busy) *in questi giorni.*
   a. *sempre*
   b. *occupato*
   c. *nuovo*

9. *Si* _____ (know) *loro?*
   a. *conosciuti*
   b. *conoscono*
   c. *conoscerla*

10. *Con chi ho il piacere di* _____ (speak)?
    a. *parlare*
    b. *avere*
    c. *conoscere*

11. *Ecco il mio* _____ (address) *ed il mio numero di telefono.*
    a. *giorno*
    b. *biglietto*
    c. *indirizzo*

12. *Ci vedremo uno di questi* _____ (days).
    a. *giorni*
    b. *molto*
    c. *settimana*

13. *Lei ha la* _____ (mine).
    a. *molto*
    b. *mia*
    c. *giorno*

14. _____ (What) *dice?*
    a. *Come*
    b. *Quando*
    c. *Che*

15. _____ (Why) *è andata via?*
    a. *Che cosa*
    b. *Perchè*
    c. *Quanto*

16. _____ (How) *si dice questo in italiano?*
    a. *Come*
    b. *Quando*
    c. *Nessuno*

17. _____ (How much) *denaro desidera?*
    a. *A chi*
    b. *Quanto*
    c. *Di chi*
18. _____ (Who) *ha il suo vino?*
    a. *Chi*
    b. *Di chi*
    c. *Quale*
19. _____ (Where is) *il suo amico?*
    a. *Dovè*
    b. *Come*
    c. *Chi*
20. _____ (When) *verrà suo fratello?*
    a. *Chi*
    b. *Quale*
    c. *Quando*

ANSWERS

1—b; 2—a; 3—c; 4—a; 5—b; 6—c; 7—a; 8—b; 9—b;
10—a; 11—c; 12—a; 13—b; 14—c; 15—b; 16—a; 17—b;
18—a; 19—a; 20—c.

SUPPLEMENTAL VOCABULARY 6: AT SCHOOL

school	*la scuola*
university	*l'università*
classroom	*la classe*
course	*il corso*
teacher	*l'insegnante, il maestro/la maestra* (nursery and elementary school)
professor	*il professore/la professoressa* (from junior high to university)
student	*lo studente/la studentessa*

subject	*la materia*
notebook	*il quaderno*
textbook	*il libro (di testo)*
math	*la matematica*
history	*la storia*
chemistry	*la chimica*
biology	*la biologia*
literature	*la letteratura*
language	*la lingua*
art	*l' arte* (f.)
music	*la musica*
gym	*la palestra*
recess	*la vacanza*
test	*l' esame* (m.), *il test*
grade	*il voto*
report card	*la scheda*
diploma	*il diploma*
degree	*il diploma* (high school), *la laurea* (college, university)
difficult/easy	*difficile/facile*
to study	*studiare*
to learn	*imparare*
to pass	*passare (l' esame)*
to fail	*essere bocciato*

LESSON 28

A.   IT'S GOOD, IT'S WONDERFUL

Buono(-a).   Good. (*masc., fem.*)
È buono.   It's good.

Molto buono.	Very good.
È molto buono.	It's very good.
È eccellente.	It's excellent.
È stupendo.	It's wonderful.
È magnifico.	It's excellent. It's wonderful.
È ammirabile.	It's excellent. It's admirable.
È perfetto.	It's perfect.
È fantastico.	It's great. *(fem.)*
È forte.	It's cool.
È di moda.	It's in (trendy).
È giusto.	It's correct.
Non c'è male.	It's not bad.
Va bene?	Is it all right?
Molto bene.	Very well.
Molto buono.	Very good.
È bella.	She's beautiful.
È bellissima.	She's very beautiful.
È molto carina.	She's very pretty, cute.
È attraente.	She's attractive.
È bello.	He's handsome.
È galante.	He's charming.
È carino.	He's cute.
È bravo.	He's a great guy.
È brava.	She's a good sport.
È molto alla mano.	She (He) is a good sport/down to earth.

B.   It's Not Good, It's Worthless

Non è buono(-a).	It's not good. It's no good. *(masc., fem.)*
Non è molto buono.	It's not very good.
Quello non è buono.	That's not good.

Questo non è giusto.	This isn't right.
Questo non è corretto.	This isn't correct. This is wrong.
È male.	It's bad.
È molto male.	It's very bad.
È pessimo.	That's very bad. That's the worst.
È fatto malissimo.	It is done very badly.
È veramente cattivo.	It's really (truly) bad.
Non mi interessa.	I don't care. It doesn't interest me.
Questo non vale niente.	That's worthless.
Non serve a nulla.	It's worthless. It's good for nothing.
Uffa! Che noia!	What a drag!
È orribile!	It's horrible!
È pessimo!	It's the worst!
Che schifo!	How disgusting!

QUIZ 26

1. *Va bene.*
2. *Molto bene.*
3. *È eccellente.*
4. *Non c'è male.*
5. *È male.*
6. *Che peccato!*
7. *È molto carina.*
8. *Non serve a nulla.*
9. *Che disgrazia!*
10. *È stupendo.*

a. It's excellent.
b. She's very pretty.
c. That's worthless.
d. What a pity!
e. How unfortunate!
f. It's wonderful!
g. It's all right.
h. That's bad.
i. Very well.
j. It's not bad.

ANSWERS

1—g; 2—i; 3—a; 4—j; 5—h; 6—d; 7—b; 8—c; 9—e; 10—f.

LESSON 29

A. I LIKE IT

Mi piace . . .	I like . . . (It pleases me . . .)
Mi piace molto.	I like it (him, her) a lot.
Mi piace moltissimo.	I like it (him, her) very much.
Mi piace quello.	I like that.
Lei mi piace.	I like her./I like you (*pol.*).
Mi piacciono molto.	I like them a lot.
La musica mi piace molto.	I love music.
Le piace?	Do you like it?
Non Le piace?	Don't you like it?
Le piace la frutta?	Do you like fruit?
Sì, la frutta mi piace.	Yes, I like fruit.
Non mi piace.	I don't like it.
Non mi piace molto.	I don't like it very much.
No, la frutta non mi piace.	No, I don't like fruit.
Le piace il cioccolato?	Do you like chocolate?
Le piace l'America?	Do you like America?
Le piace la cucina italiana?	Do you like Italian food?
Le piace l'Italia?	Do you like Italy?
Le è piaciuta l'Italia?	Did you like Italy?
L'Italia mi è piaciuta.	I liked Italy.
Crede che la casa gli piacerà?	Do you think they'll like the house?
Vi piace la mia camera?	How do you all like my room?
Non mi piace.	I don't like it.
Non mi piace molto.	I don't like it very much.
Se Le piace.	If you like it.
Quando Le piace.	Whenever you like.
Quando desidera.	Whenever you want.

Notice that the Italian for "I like fruit" is *mi piace la frutta* (fruit is pleasing to me). That is, the word which is the object in English is the subject in Italian. "I like spaghetti" is *mi piacciono gli spaghetti* (spaghetti is pleasing to me). Here the verb is plural because the subject *(gli spaghetti)* is plural.

B. I DON'T CARE

Non m'importa.	I don't care.
Non me ne importa niente.	I couldn't care less.
Non me ne importa un fico secco.	I don't give a damn.
Non m'importa affatto.	I don't care at all.
Chi se ne importa?	Who cares?
Non importa.	It doesn't make any difference.

C. I HAD A GOOD TIME

Mi sono divertito(-a).	I had a good time
Ci siamo divertiti un sacco!	We had a blast!
Non mi sono divertito(-a).	I didn't have a good time.
È stata una perdita di tempo. È stato uno spreco di tempo.	It was a waste of time.
Divertiti! Buon divertimento!	Have a good time! *(singular)*
Divertitevi! Buon divertimento!	Have a good time! *(plural)*

QUIZ 27

1. *Le piace la cucina italiana?*   a. I don't like it very much.
2. *Le piace?*   b. Do you like my room?
3. *Mi piace molto.*   c. Do you like Italy?
4. *Le piace la frutta?*   d. If you like.

5. *Quando Le piace.*   e. Don't you like it?
6. *Le piace l'Italia?*   f. I like it very much.
7. *Non le piace?*   g. Do you like it?
8. *Se le piace.*   h. Whenever you like.
9. *Non mi piace molto.*   i. Do you like Italian food?
10. *Le piace la mia camera?*   j. Do you like fruit?

ANSWERS
1—i; 2—g; 3—f; 4—j; 5—h; 6—c; 7—e; 8—d; 9—a; 10—b.

SUPPLEMENTAL VOCABULARY 7: SPORTS AND RECREATION

soccer	*il calcio, il futbol*
basketball	*la pallacanestro*
baseball	*il baseball*
american football	*il futbol americano*
hockey	*l'hockey su ghiaccio*
tennis	*il tennis*
biking	*il ciclismo*
swimming	*il nuoto*
game	*la partita*
team	*la squadra*
stadium	*lo stadio*
coach	*l'allenatore/l'allenatrice*
player	*il giocatore/la giocatrice*
champion	*il campione/la campionessa*
ball	*la palla, il pallone*
(to go) hiking	*camminare in montagna*
(to go) camping	*fare il campeggio, andare in campeggio*
to play (a sport)	*praticare uno sport*
to play (a game)	*giocare a*
to win	*vincere*

to lose	*perdere*
to draw/tie	*fare pari, pareggiare*
cards	*(giocare a) carte*
pool/billiards	*(giocare a) biliardo*

LESSON 30

A. IN, TO, FROM, ETC. (PREPOSITIONS)

Abito in Italia.	I live in Italy.
Sono stato(-a) a Roma.	I've been in Rome.
Vado a Roma.	I'm going to Rome.
Vengo da Roma.	I come from Rome.
Parto per Roma.	I'm leaving for Rome.
Lui va verso Roma.	He's going toward Rome.
Sono andat*o*(-a) fino a Roma.	I went as far as Rome.
Vado in Europa.	I am going to Europe.

1. *A* = To, In

a destra	to the right
a sinistra	to the left
due a due	two by two
poco a poco	little by little
a piedi	on foot
a mano	by hand
a mezzogiorno	at noon
a mezzanotte	at midnight
Si sono seduti a tavola.	They sat down at the table.
all' italiana	in the Italian manner
A domani.	Until tomorrow.
A presto.	See you soon. (Until soon.)
A più tardi.	See you later. (Until later.)

Arrivederci.	Good-bye.
Alla prossima volta.	Until next time.

2. *Con* = With

Io sono andato(-a) con Giovanni.	I went with John.
Lui lo ha scritto con una matita.	He wrote it with a pencil.

3. *Di* = Of, From

È di mio fratello.	It's my brother's.
Io sono di Roma.	I am from Rome.
È fatto di legno.	It's made of wood.
di giorno	by day, in the daytime
di nuovo	again (of new)

4. *In* = In

Ho vissuto in Italia per vari anni.	I lived in Italy for several years.
Il treno partirà in orario.	The train will leave on time.
Venga in salotto.	Come into the parlor. *(pol.)*
in quella direzione	in that direction

5. *Fino a* = Up to, Until

fino a Milano	up to (as far as) Milano
Io sono salito(-a) fino al quinto piano.	I walked up to the fifth floor.

6. *Verso* = Toward, Around (Approximately)

Lei camminava verso il parco.	She was walking toward (in the direction of) the park.
Ha cominciato a piovere verso mezzanotte.	It started to rain around midnight.

7. *Da* = From, Since

da Napoli a Capri	from Naples to Capri
da quando l'ho visto	since I saw him; since the time when I saw him

8. *Per* = For, Through, In place of

L'ho comprato per un dollaro.	I bought it for a dollar.
Gli ho dato un dollaro per questo.	I gave him a dollar for this.
Lui mi ha dato il suo libro per il mio.	He exchanged books with me. (He gave me his book for mine.)
Noi siamo passati per Roma.	We passed through Rome.
Il treno passa per Roma.	The train passes through Rome.
Io vado per Lei.	I'll go for (in place of) you.
Io sarò in viaggio per due anni.	I'll be away traveling for two years.

9. *Sopra* = On, Above, Over

sopra la tavola	above the table
Lei aveva un cappotto sopra le spalle.	She had a coat on her back.

10. *Su* = On, On top of

La tovaglia è sulla tavola.	The tablecloth is on the table.
Ha un velo sui capelli.	She has a veil on her hair.

B. OTHER PREPOSITIONAL EXPRESSIONS

a causa di	on account of
alla fine	eventually

disposto(-a) a farlo	in favor of doing it
di conseguenza	consequently, as a result
di notte	at night
invece di questo	instead of this
in generale	in general
nel pomeriggio	during the afternoon, in the afternoon
Perchè?	Why? What is the reason?
per ora	for the time being
per esempio	for example
per quanto riguarda	in regard to
per quella ragione	for that reason
Lui ha camminato per la strada.	He walked along the street.
Per amor di Dio!	For goodness' sake! For heaven's sake!
qui intorno	around here
dalla porta	through the door
dalla finestra	through the window

C. WORD STUDY

ballo	ball
biglietto	ticket
formaggio	cheese
civile	civil
educazione	education, manners
efficiente	efficient
logico	logical
tavola	table

QUIZ 28

1. *a mezzogiorno*   a. on foot
2. *poco a poco*   b. one by one

3. *a destra*   c. I come from Rome.
4. *all' italiana*   d. It's made of wood.
5. *con*   e. by day
6. *a piedi*   f. again
7. *Vengo da Roma.*   g. on the table
8. *È fatto di legno.*   h. to the right
9. *per quanto riguarda*   i. in that direction
10. *di nuovo*   j. little by little
11. *in quella direzione*   k. until tomorrow
12. *di giorno*   l. at noon
13. *a sinistra*   m. For heaven's sake!
14. *uno a uno*   n. in the Italian manner/
                                          style
15. *fino a Milano*   o. with
16. *Partirò fra due giorni.*   p. instead of
17. *sulla tavola*   q. to the left
18. *a domani*   r. in regard to
19. *invece di*   s. as far as Milano
20. *Per amor di Dio!*   t. I'm leaving in two days.

ANSWERS

1—l; 2—j; 3—h; 4—n; 5—o; 6—a; 7—c; 8—d; 9—r;
10—f; 11—i; 12—e; 13—q; 14—b; 15—s; 16—t; 17—g;
18—k; 19—p; 20—m.

QUIZ 29

1. *per esempio*   a. I gave him a dollar for
                                          this.
2. *Il treno passa per*   b. I'll be traveling for two
   Roma.   years.
3. *Siamo passati per Roma.*   c. completely
4. *per ora*   d. for that reason
5. *L' ho comprato per un*   e. around here
   dollaro.

6. *per quella ragione*   f. For goodness' sake!

7. *Io sarò in viaggio per*   g. at last
    due anni.

8. *completamente*   h. for example

9. *Io gli ho dato un*   i. I am not in favor of
    dollaro per questo.

10. *Per amor di Dio!*   j. for the time being

11. *alla fine*   k. I bought it for a dollar.

12. *Lui è entrato dalla*   l. The train passes through
     porta.   Rome.

13. *qui intorno*   m. I take this instead of
                                that.

14. *non sono disposto(-a)*   n. He came in through the
                                door.

15. *Prendo questo invece*   o. We passed through
     di quello.   Rome.

ANSWERS

1—h; 2—l; 3—o; 4—j; 5—k; 6—d; 7—b; 8—c; 9—a;
10—f; 11—g; 12—n; 13—e; 14—i; 15—m.

LESSON 31

A. ON THE ROAD

Scusi. Perdoni.
Excuse me. Pardon me. *(polite)*

Mi perdoni.
Pardon me. *(pol.)*

Mi scusi.
Excuse me. *(pol.)*

Qualè il nome di questo paese?
What is the name of this town?

Quanto siamo distanti da Roma?
How far are we from Rome?

Quanti chilometri ci sono da qui a Roma?
How many kilometers are there from here to Rome?

È a dieci chilometri da qui.
It's ten kilometers from here.

È a venti chilometri da qui.
It's twenty kilometers from here.

Come arrivo a Roma da qui?
How do I get to Rome from here?

Segua questa strada.
Follow this road. *(pol.)*

Come si arriva a questo posto?
How do you get to this place?

È molto lontano?
Is it very far?

Qualè la via più breve per andare a Torino?
What's the shortest way to get to Turin?

Quale strada devo prendere?
Which road should I take?

Dov'è il parcheggio?
Where is the parking lot?

Supplemental Vocabulary 8:
Travel and Tourism

tourist	*il/la turista*
hotel	*l' albergo, l' hotel (m.)*
youth hostel	*l' ostello*
reception desk	*la reception, l' accettazione*
to check in	*registrarsi (all' hotel)*
to check out	*pagare il conto (dell' hotel)*
reservation	*(fare) la prenotazione*
passport	*il passaporto*
tour bus	*il pullman*
guided tour	*il viaggio organizzato*
camera	*la macchina fotografica (digitale)*
information center	*il centro informazioni*
map	*la piantina, la cartina, la mappa*
brochure	*l' opuscolo*
monument	*il monumento*
to go sightseeing	*visitare*
to take a picture	*fare una fotografia/delle fotografie*
Can you take our picture?	*Può farci una foto(grafia)?*

B. Walking Around

Può dirmi come posso arrivare a questo indirizzo?
Can you tell me how I can get to this address?

Può dirmi come posso arrivare a questo posto?
Can you tell me how I can get to this place?

Come si chiama questa strada?
What is the name of this street?

Puo indicarmi dov'è Via Veneto?
Can you direct me to Veneto Street?

Dov'è questo indirizzo?
Where is this address?

È qui vicino Via Barberini?
Is Barberini Street near here?

Penso di essermi smarrito(-a).
I think I'm lost.

Dov'è un telefono pubblico?
Where is there a public phone?

Può dirmi dov'è questa strada?
Can you tell me where this street is?

Dov'è Via Rossini?
Where is Rossini Street?

È lontano da qui?
Is it far from here?

È vicino?
Is it near?

È la terza strada a destra.
It's the third street on the right.

Vada per questa strada.
Go this way. *(pol.)*

Vada avanti diritto.
Go straight ahead. *(pol.)*

Vada fino all'angolo e volti a sinistra.
Go to the corner and turn left. *(pol.)*

Prenda la prima strada a sinistra.
Take the first street to the left. *(pol.)*

Volti a destra.
Turn right. *(pol.)*

Dov'è la Questura?
Where is the Police Station?

Dov'è il Municipio?
Where is City Hall?

SUPPLEMENTAL VOCABULARY 9: NATURE

tree	*l'albero*
flower	*il fiore*
forest	*la foresta*
mountain	*la montagna*
field	*il campo*
river	*il fiume*
lake	*il lago*
ocean	*l'oceano*
sea	*il mare*
beach	*la spiaggia*
desert	*il deserto*
rock	*la roccia*
sand	*la sabbia*
sky	*il cielo*
sun	*il sole*
moon	*la luna*
star	*la stella*
water	*l'acqua*
land	*la terra*

plant	*la pianta*
hill	*la collina*
pond	*lo stagno*

C. Taking a Bus, Train, Taxi, or Subway

Dov'è la fermata dell'autobus?
Where is the bus stop?

A quale fermata scendo?
At what stop do I get off?

Si ferma qui l'autobus?
Does the bus stop here?

Dove scendo?
Where do I get off?

Dov'è la stazione ferroviaria?
Where is the railroad station?

Quanto è lontana da qui la stazione?
How far is the station from here?

Siamo ancora lontani dalla stazione?
Are we still far from the station?

Dove si prende il treno per Roma?
Where do you get the train for Rome?

Da quale binario parte il treno per Roma?
From which track does the train for Rome leave?

A quale binario arriva il treno da Roma?
At which track does the Rome train arrive?

Dov'è l'ufficio informazioni?
Where is the information office?

Vuole darmi per favore un orario ferroviario?
Could you please give me a timetable?

Qualè il treno per Roma?
Which is the train for Rome?

È questo il treno per Roma?
Is this the train for Rome?

Dove si prende il treno per Roma?
Where do you get the train for Rome?

Al binario due.
On track two.

Quando parte il treno per Roma?
When does the train for Rome leave?

Il treno è appena partito.
The train just left.

Il treno sta per partire.
The train is about to leave.

Quando parte il prossimo treno?
When does the next train leave?

Dov'è la biglietteria?
Where is the ticket window?

Mi dia un biglietto di andata per Roma.
Give me a one-way ticket to Rome. *(pol.)*

Un biglietto di andata e ritorno per Roma, per favore.
A round-trip ticket to Rome, please.

Di prima o di seconda classe?
First or second class?

Prima classe.
First class.

Quanto costa?
How much does it cost?

Tre euro.
Three euros.

Quanto tempo ci vuole per arrivare?
How long does it take to get there?

Un po' più di un'ora.
A little more than an hour.

È occupato questo posto?
Is this seat taken?

Posso mettere la mia valigia qui?
May I put my suitcase here?

Che stazione è questa?
What station is this?

Per quanto tempo ci fermiamo qui?
How long do we stop here?

Devo cambiare treno qui?
Do I change trains here?

Questo treno si ferma a Roma?
Does this train stop in Rome?

Tassì! *(Taxi!)*
Taxi!

È libero?
Are you free (unoccupied)?

Mi porti a questo indirizzo.
Take me to this address. *(pol.)*

Quanto Le devo?
How much do I owe you?

Si ferma qui il tram?
Does the streetcar stop here?

A che fermata devo scendere?
At what stop do I get off?

Dov'è la stazione della metropolitana più vicina?
Where is the nearest subway station?

QUIZ 30

1. *Qualè la via più breve per andare a . . . ?*
2. *Da dove posso telefonare?*
3. *Dov' è questa strada?*
4. *Mi porti a questo indirizzo.*
5. *Quanto è lontana la stazione?*

a. How far is the station?
b. How do you get to this place?
c. Can you direct me to . . . Street?
d. Does the bus stop here?
e. At which stop do I get off?

6. *Posso usare il telefono?*   f. Where can I make a
                                     phone call?

7. *Può indicarmi dov'è*   g. Where is this street?
   via ... ?

8. *A quale fermata devo*   h. What's the shortest way
   scendere?   to get to ... ?

9. *Come si arriva a questo* i. Take me to this address.
   posto?

10. *Si ferma qui l'autobus?*   j. May I use the phone?

ANSWERS

1—h; 2—f; 3—g; 4—i; 5—a; 6—j; 7—c; 8—e; 9—b;
10—d.

SUPPLEMENTAL VOCABULARY 10: AROUND TOWN

town	*il paese* (small town), *la cittadina* (town)
city	*la città*
village	*il paesino* (small village), *il paese* (village)
car	*la macchina*
bus	*l'autobus* (m.)
train	*il treno*
taxi	*il taxi*
subway/metro	*il metrò* (in Milan), *la metro* (in Rome)
traffic	*il traffico*
building	*l'edificio, il palazzo* (old)
apartment building	*il condominio*
library	*la biblioteca*
restaurant	*il ristorante*
store	*il negozio*
street	*la strada*
park	*il parco*
train station	*la stazione (dei treni)*

airport	*l' aeroporto*
airplane	*l' aereo*
intersection	*l' incrocio*
lamp post	*il lampione*
street light	*il semaforo*
bank	*la banca*
church	*la chiesa*
temple	*il tempio*
mosque	*la moschea*
sidewalk	*il marciapiede*
bakery	*la pasticceria*
butcher shop	*la macelleria*
café/coffee shop	*il bar, il caffè*
drugstore/pharmacy	*la farmacia*
supermarket	*il supermercato*
market	*il mercato*
shoe store	*il negozio di scarpe*
clothing store	*il negozio di abbigliamento*
electronics store	*il negozio di elettronica*
bookstore	*la libreria*
department store	*il grande magazzino*
shopping mall	*il centro acquisti/ commerciale*
mayor	*il sindaco*
city hall, municipal building	*il municipio*
to buy	*comprare*
to go shopping	*fare le spese*
near/far	*vicino/lontano*
urban	*urbano*
suburban	*periferico*
rural	*rurale*

LESSON 32

A. WRITING AND MAILING LETTERS

Vorrei scrivere una lettera.
I'd like to write a letter.

Mi può dare un po' di carta?
Could you let me have (give me) some paper? *(pol.)*

Qui c'è carta e una penna.
Here is some paper and a pen.

Ha una matita?
Do you have a pencil?

Ha una penna?
Do you have a pen?

Ha un foglio di carta?
Do you have a piece (leaf) of paper?

Ha una busta?
Do you have an envelope?

Ha un francobollo?
Do you have a stamp?

Dove posso comprare un francobollo?
Where can I buy a stamp?

Ha un francobollo per posta aerea?
Do you have an airmail stamp?

Vado all'ufficio postale.
I'm going to the post office.

Dov'è l'ufficio postale?
Where is the post office?

Vorrei imbucare questa lettera.
I'd like to mail this letter.

Quanti francobolli occorrono per questa lettera?
How many stamps do I need on this letter?

Ho bisogno di un francobollo per posta aerea.
I need an airmail stamp.

Ecco dei francobolli.
Here are some stamps.

Un francobollo per espresso, per favore.
A special delivery stamp, please.

Dov'è la cassetta delle lettere?
Dov'è la buca delle lettere?
Where is the mailbox?

Dov'è la cassetta postale più vicina?
Where is the nearest mailbox?

All'angolo.
On the corner.

Dov'è un telefono pubblico?
Where is the public telephone office?

È nell'ufficio postale.
It's in the post office.

B. Faxes and E-mail

Devo spedire un facsìmile/*un fax*.
I have to send a fax.

Vorrei mandare un facsìmile/*un fax*.
I'd like to send a fax.

Quanto costa un facsìmile/un fax per Roma?
How much is a fax to Rome?

Da dove posso spedire un facsìmile/*un fax*?
From where can I fax?

Devo mandare un e-mail.
I have to send an e-mail message.

Posso collegarmi con internet?
Can I get on the Internet?

Avete un sito web?
Do you have a website?

Dov'è il computer?
Where is the computer?

Supplemental Vocabulary 11: Computers and the Internet

computer	*il computer*
keyboard	*la tastiera*
monitor/screen	*il monitor, lo schermo, il video*
printer	*la stampante*
mouse	*il mouse*
mouse pad	*il tappetino*

modem	*il modem*
memory	*la memoria*
cd rom	*il cd rom*
cd rom drive	*il lettore cd, il lettore cd-rom*
file	*il file, il documento*
document	*il documento*
cable	*il cavo*
internet	*internet*
website	*il sito web*
webpage	*la web page, la pagina web*
e-mail	*l'email (f.), la posta elettronica*
address book	*la rubrica*
to attach a file	*allegare un documento*
to open a file	*aprire un documento*
send now	*invia ora*
send later	*invia più tardi*
reply	*rispondi al mittente*
send and receive	*invia e ricevi*
attachment	*l'allegato (m.)*
to forward	*inoltrare*
to reply	*rispondere*
to download	*scaricare*
to click	*cliccare*
to close a file	*chiudere un file, chiudere un documento*
to attach a file	*allegare un file/un documento*
to send an e-mail	*mandare un' email*
to send a file	*inviare un file, inviare un documento*
to delete	*cancellare, eliminare*
to save a document	*salvare un documento*

chatroom	*la chatroom, la stanza di chat*
web log (blog)	*il web log*
instant message	*il messaggio immediato*
attachment	*l'allegato*

C. TELEPHONING

C'è un telefono?
Is there a phone here?

Da dove posso telefonare?
Where can I make a phone call?

Dov'è il telefono?
Where is the telephone?

Dov'è la cabina telefonica?
Where is the phone booth?

Nell'atrio dell'albergo.
In the hotel lobby.

Posso usare il Suo cellulare?
May I use your phone?

Sicuro! Si accomodi!
Of course! Go ahead! *(pol.)*

Posso fare una chiamata interurbana?
Can I make a long distance call?

Quanto costa una telefonata per Roma?
How much is a phone call to Rome?

Posso avere il numero otto, sette, cinque, otto, due, quattro, tre?
May I have 87-58-243?

Aspetti un momento.
Hold on a minute. *(pol.)*

La linea è occupata.
The line is busy.

Centralino, Lei mi ha dato il numero sbagliato.
Operator, you gave me the wrong number.

Non risponde.
There is no answer.

Posso parlare con il signor Ferri?
May I speak to Mr. Ferri?

In persona.
Speaking.

Questo è il signor Villanova che parla.
This is Mr. Villanova speaking.

Parlo con il signor Ferri?
Am I speaking with Mr. Ferri?

Sono io.
Speaking. (It is I.)

Con chi parlo?
Who is this? (With whom am I speaking?)

Con il signor Ferri.
With Mr. Ferri.

D. WORD STUDY

computer (*m.*)	computer
portatile (*m.*)	laptop/portable computer
stampante	printer
schermo	screen
telefono cellulare; telefonino	cellular phone
segreteria telefonica	answering machine
posta vocale	voice mail
lasciare un messaggio	to leave a message
e-mail; posta elettronica	e-mail

QUIZ 31

1. *Dove posso comprare un francobollo?*
2. *La linea è occupata.*
3. *Sono io.*
4. *Ha una busta?*
5. *Posso fare una chiamata interurbana?*
6. *All' angolo.*
7. *Non risponde.*
8. *Aspetti un momento.*
9. *il numero sbagliato*
10. *Vorrei mandare un facsìmile/fax.*

a. Speaking.
b. Can I make a long distance call?
c. On the corner.
d. There is no answer.
e. Where can I buy a stamp?
f. the wrong number
g. I'd like to send a fax.
h. Do you have an envelope?
i. Hold on a minute.
j. The line is busy.

1—e; 2—j; 3—a; 4—h; 5—b; 6—c; 7—d; 8—i; 9—f; 10—g.

SUPPLEMENTAL VOCABULARY 12: IN THE OFFICE

office	*l' ufficio*
desk	*la scrivania*
computer	*il computer*
telephone	*il telefono; il cellulare, il telefonino*
fax machine	*il fax*
book shelf	*lo scaffale (dei libri)*
file cabinet	*lo schedario*
file	*la cartella*
boss	*il capo, la capa*
colleague	*il/la collega*
employee	*l' impiegato*
staff	*lo staff*
company	*la ditta*
business	*il business*
factory	*la fabbrica*
meeting room	*la sala delle riunioni*
meeting	*la riunione*
appointment	*l' appuntamento*
salary	*il salario*
job	*il lavoro*
busy	*occupato, impegnato*
to work	*lavorare*
to earn	*guadagnare*

LESSON 33

A.   WHAT'S YOUR NAME?

Come si chiama?
What's your name? *(pol.)*

Come ti chiami?
What's your name? *(fam.)*

Mi chiamo Giovanni Ferri.
My name is John Ferri.

Come si chiama *(lei)?*
What's her name?

Si chiama Maria Ferrari.
Her name is Maria Ferrari.

Come si chiamano?
What are their names?

Lui si chiama Giuseppe Riva e lei Anna Martini.
His name is Joseph Riva and her name is Anna Martini.

Qual'è il suo nome?
What's his (her) first name?

Il suo nome è Carlo.
His first name is Charles.

Qual'è il suo cognome?
What is his (her) last name?

Il suo cognome è Peretti.
His (her) last name is Peretti.

B.   WHERE ARE YOU FROM?

Di dov'è Lei?
Where are you from? *(pol.)*

Di dove sei *(tu)?*
Where are you from? *(fam.)*

Io sono di Roma.
I'm from Rome.

Dov'è nato (nata)?
Where were you born?

Sono nato (nata) a Roma.
I was born in Rome.

C.   HOW OLD ARE YOU?

Quanti anni ha?
How old are you?

Ho ventiquattro anni.
I'm twenty-four.

Compirò ventiquattro anni a settembre.
I'll be twenty-four in September.

Sono nato il diciannove agosto millenovecentosessanta.
I was born August 19, 1960.

Quando è il Suo compleanno?
When is your birthday?

Il mio compleanno è fra due settimane, il ventitrè gennaio.
My birthday is in two weeks, January 23.

D. Professions

Qual è il Suo mestiere/*la Sua professione*?
What do you do?

Sono artista.
I'm an artist.

Cosa fa Suo padre?
What does your father do?

Cosa fa Sua madre?
What does your mother do?

È avvocato.
He's (she's) a lawyer.

È architetto.
He's (she's) an architect.

È insegnante.
He's (she's) a teacher.

È professore d'università. (È professoressa d'università.)
He's (she's) a university professor.

È dottore. (È dottoressa.)
He's (she's) a doctor.

È uomo d'affari.
He's a businessman.

È una donna d'affari.
She's a businesswoman.

È agricoltore. (È agricoltrice.)
He's (she's) a farmer.

È un funzionario dello Stato.
He's (she's) a government worker.

È operaio. (È operaia.)
He's (she's) a worker.

Lavora in una fabbrica di automobili.
He (she) works in an automobile factory.

SUPPLEMENTAL VOCABULARY 13: JOBS

police man/woman	*poliziotto/donna poliziotto*
lawyer	*avvocato/avvocato*
doctor	*dottore/dottoressa*
engineer	*ingegnere/ingegnere*
businessman/woman	*uomo d'affari/donna d'affari*
salesman/woman	*venditore/venditrice*
teacher	*insegnante/insegnante*
professor	*professore/professoressa*
banker	*banchiere/banchiera*
architect	*architetto/architetto*
veterinarian	*veterinario/veterinaria*
dentist	*dentista/dentista*
stay-at-home dad/mom	*casalingo/casalinga*
carpenter	*falegname/falegname*
construction worker	*muratore/muratrice*
taxi driver	*taxista/taxista*
artist	*artista/artista*
writer	*scrittore/scrittrice*
plumber	*idraulico/idraulica*
electrician	*elettricista/elettricista*
journalist	*giornalista/giornalista*
actor/actress	*attore/attrice*
musician	*musicista/musicista*

farmer	*contadino/contadina*
secretary/assistant	*segretario/segretaria,*
	assistente/assistente
unemployed	*disoccupato/disoccupata*
retired	*pensionato/pensionata*
full-time	*a tempo pieno*
part-time	*part time*
steady job	*lavoro fisso*
temp. job	*lavoro temporaneo*

E. FAMILY MATTERS

Ha parenti qui?
Do you have any relatives here?

Quanti fratelli ha?
How many brothers do you have?

Ho due fratelli.
I have two brothers.

Il maggiore ha ventidue anni.
The older one is twenty-two.

Studia all'Università.
He is at the University.

Il minore ha quindici anni.
The younger one is fifteen.

Lui frequenta l'ultimo anno del liceo.
He's in his last year of high school.

Quante sorelle ha?
How many sisters do you have?

Ho una sorella.
I have one sister.

Ha nove anni.
She's nine.

Frequenta la scuola elementare.
She goes to grammar (elementary) school.

Vive qui tutta la Sua famiglia?
Does your whole family live here?

Tutta la mia famiglia, meno i miei nonni.
My whole family, except my grandparents.

Loro vivono in una villa di campagna vicino a Firenze.
They live in a country home near Florence.

È imparentato(-a) con il signor Villanova/È parente del signor Villanova?
Are you related to Mr. Villanova?

È mio zio.
He's my uncle.

È mio cugino.
He's my cousin.

È imparentato(-a) con la signora Rossi/È parente della signora Rossi?
Are you related to Mrs. Rossi?

È mia zia.
She's my aunt.

È mia cugina.
She's my cousin.

F. WORD STUDY

ansioso	anxious
consolato	consulate
differente	different
difficile	difficult
dottore	doctor
festa	feast
futuro	future
lingua	language
visita	visit

QUIZ 32

1. *Ho una sorella.*	a. What is his (her) first name?
2. *Di dov' è Lei?*	b. I'm twenty-four.
3. *Quanti anni ha Lei?*	c. Where are you from?
4. *Qual' è il suo nome?*	d. What are their names?
5. *È mia zia.*	e. She's my aunt.
6. *È insegnante.*	f. I have one sister.
7. *Come si chiamano?*	g. Are you related to Mr. Villanova?
8. *Sono nato(-a) a Roma.*	h. How old are you?
9. *Ho ventiquattro anni.*	i. I was born in Rome.
10. *È imparentato(-a) con il signor Villanova?*	j. He's (she's) a teacher.

ANSWERS

1—f; 2—c; 3—h; 4—a; 5—e; 6—j; 7—d; 8—i; 9—b; 10—g.

SUPPLEMENTAL VOCABULARY 14: FAMILY AND RELATIONSHIPS

mother	*madre*
father	*padre*
son	*figlio*
daughter	*figlia*
sister	*sorella*
baby	*bambino*
brother	*fratello*
husband	*marito*
wife	*moglie*
aunt	*zia*
uncle	*zio*
grandmother	*nonna*
grandfather	*nonno*
cousin	*cugino*
mother-in-law	*suocera*
father-in-law	*suocero*
stepmother	*la moglie di mio padre*
stepfather	*il marito di mia madre*
stepson	*il figlio di mia moglie/di mio marito*
stepdaughter	*la figlia di mia moglie/di mio marito*
boyfriend	*il mio ragazzo*
girlfriend	*la mia ragazza*
fiancé(e)	*il fidanzato/la fidanzata*
friend	*amico/amica*
relative	*parente*
to love	*innamorato*
to know (a person)	*conoscere*
to meet (a person)	*conoscere* (for the first time), *incontrare, vedere* (casually)

to marry (someone)	*sposarsi (con qualcuno)*
to divorce (someone)	*divorziarsi (da qualcuno)*
to get a divorce	*divorziare*
to inherit	*ereditare*

LESSON 34

A. SHOPPING

1. **Quanto costa questo?**
   How much is this?

2. **Trenta euro.**
   Thirty euros.

3. **È piuttosto caro.**
   That's rather expensive.

   Non ha niente di più economico?
   Don't you have anything cheaper?

4. **Dello stesso modello?**
   In the same style?

5. **Lo stesso modello o qualche cosa di simile.**
   The same style or something similar.

6. **C'è questo.**
   There's this.

7. **Non ha nient'altro da farmi vedere?**
   Don't you have anything else you could show me?

8. **Meno caro?**
   Less expensive?

9. **Se è possibile.**
   If (it's) possible.

10. **Forse Le piace questo?**
    Perhaps you like this?

11. **Dipende dal prezzo.**
    That depends on the price.

12. **Questo costa diciassette euro.**
    This one is seventeen euros.

13. **Mi piace più dell'altro.**
    I like it better than the other one.

14. **È più economico.**
    It's more affordable.

15. **Com'è questo? È più economico o più caro?**
    How about this? Is it cheaper or more expensive?

16. **È più caro.**
    It's more expensive.

17. **Non ha altro assortimento?**
    Don't you have anything else in stock?

18. **Spero di ricevere presto nuovi modelli.**
    I'm hoping to receive some new styles soon.

19. **Fra quanto?**
    How soon?

20. **Da un giorno all'altro.**
    Any day now.

    Può ripassare verso la fine della settimana?
    Can you drop in toward the end of the week?

21. **Lo farò . . . Quanto costano questi?**
    I'll do that . . . What's the price of these?

22. **Due euro al paio.**
    Two euros a pair.

23. **Me ne dia una dozzina.**
    Let me have a dozen. *(pol.)*

24. **Vuole portarli con sè?**
    Will you take them with you? Will you take them yourself?

25. **Preferisco che me li mandi a casa.**
    I'd rather have you send them to my house.

26. **L'indirizzo è sempre lo stesso?**
    Is the address still the same?

27. **È lo stesso.**
    It's the same.

28. **ArrivederLa.**
    Good-bye.

NOTES

3. *È piuttosto caro* = That's rather expensive. *Molto caro* = very expensive. *Economico,* or *a buon mercato* =

cheap. *Più economico* = cheaper. *Molto economico* = very cheap.

5. *Qualche cosa di simile* = something (of) similar.

7. *Da farmi vedere* = To let me see. You can also use *mostrarmi*.

19. *Fra quanto?* Idiomatic expression for "How soon?" It can also be expressed by *Fra quanto tempo?* (In how much time/long?)

20. *Da un giorno all' altro* = from one day to the other.

21. *Lo farò.* (I will do that.) Future of the verb *fare*.

23. *Me ne dia una dozzina.* (Give me a dozen of them.) *Dia* is the polite imperative of *dare*.

24. *Con se* = with yourself.
    Mandi: subjunctive of *mandare*.

28. *ArrivederLa* is used instead of *arrivederci* because the speaker is using the polite mode of address.

QUIZ 33

1. *È abbastanza* _____ (expensive).
    a. *costa*
    b. *questo*
    c. *caro*
2. *Ha nulla di più* _____ (cheap)?
    a. *qualità*
    b. *prezzo*
    c. *economico*

3. *Della* _____ (same) *qualità.*
   a. *qualche cosa*
   b. *stessa*
   c. *più*

4. _____ (Less) *caro.*
   a. *Più*
   b. *Meno*
   c. *Stesso*

5. *Mi piace* _____ (more) *dell' altro.*
   a. *come*
   b. *più*
   c. *vale*

6. *Non* _____ (have) *maggiore assortimento?*
   a. *ha*
   b. *caro*
   c. *altro*

7. *Spero di* _____ (receive) *notizie.*
   a. *scelta*
   b. *tranquillo*
   c. *ricevere*

8. *A* _____ (when)?
   a. *assortimento*
   b. *caro*
   c. *quando*

9. *Allo stesso* _____ (address)?
   a. *indirizzo*
   b. *domicilio*
   c. *spedire*

ANSWERS

1—c; 2—c; 3—b; 4—b; 5—b; 6—a; 7—c; 8—c; 9—a.

SUPPLEMENTAL VOCABULARY 15: CLOTHING

shirt	*la camicia*
pants	*i pantaloni*
jeans	*i blue jeans*
tee shirt	*la maglietta*
shoe(s)	*le scarpe*
sock(s)	*le calze/i calzini*
belt	*la cintura*
sneakers, tennis shoes	*le scarpe da ginnastica, le scarpe da tennis, gli sneakers*
dress	*il vestito*
skirt	*la gonna*
blouse	*la camicetta*
suit	*l'abito da uomo* (men), *il tailleur (pantalone)* (women)
hat	*il cappello*
glove(s)	*i guanti*
scarf	*il foulard* (if square), *la sciarpa* (if long)
jacket	*la giacca*
coat	*il cappotto* (if to the knees or longer), *la giacca/il giaccone* (if shorter)
earring	*gli orecchini*
bracelet	*il braccialetto*
necklace	*la collana*
eyeglasses	*gli occhiali*
sunglasses	*gli occhiali da sole*
watch	*l'orologio*
ring	*l'anello*
underpants	*le mutande* (boxers), *gli slip* (briefs), *le mutandine* (for women)

undershirt	*la canottiera*
bra	*il reggiseno*
bathing trunks	*il costume da bagno*
bathing suit	*il costume da bagno*
bikini	*il bichini*
pyjamas	*il pigiama*
cotton	*(di) cotone*
leather	*(di) pelle*
silk	*(di) seta*
wool	*(di) lana*
size	*misura* (shirts), *taglia* (dresses, pants), *numero* (shoes)
to wear	*portare*

LESSON 35

A. BREAKFAST IN A RESTAURANT

1. P[1]: **Hai fame?**
   Are you hungry? (Do you have an appetite?)

2. Sig: **Sì, ho fame.**
   I certainly am.

3. P: **Cameriere! Cameriere!**
   Waiter! Waiter!

4. C: **Cosa desidera?**
   What would you like?

---

[1] "P" represents Mr. Paoli. "Sig" stands for *Signora* (his wife), and "C" for *Cameriere* (Waiter).

5. P: **Vorremmo fare colazione.**
We'd like to have breakfast.

6. Sig: **Cosa ci può servire?**
What can you serve us?

7. C: **Caffelatte, tè con limone o con latte, cioccolata . . .**
Coffee with milk, tea with lemon or with milk, hot chocolate . . .

8. Sig: **Con che lo servite?**
What do you serve with it?

9. C: **Con panini, paste, biscotti . . .**
Rolls, pastry, cookies . . .

10. Sig: **C'è del burro?**
Is there any butter?

11. C: **Sì, signora.**
Yes, madam.

12. Sig: **Mi porta una tazza di caffè con latte, per piacere.**
Bring me a cup of coffee with milk. *(pol.)*

13. P: **Anche a me. E mi porti pure due uova fritte.**
The same for me. And bring me also two fried eggs. *(pol.)*

14. Sig: **Cameriere, mi porta un tovagliolo per favore ?**
Waiter, would you please bring me a napkin? *(pol.)*

15. P: **Per me, una forchetta.**
And a fork for me.

16. Sig: **Per favore ci porta ancora un pò di zucchero.**
    Please bring us a little more sugar. *(pol.)*

17. P: **E poi ci porti il conto ... Ecco qui ... tenga il resto.**
    And then let's have a check ... Here you are ... keep the change. *(pol.)*

18. C: **Molte grazie, signore.**
    Thank you, sir.

NOTES

Breakfast is called *la prima colazione* or simply *colazione.* *Il pranzo* = lunch. *La cena* = dinner.

4. *Che cosa, cosa,* and *che* all mean "what."

5. *Vorremmo,* conditional of *volere* (because it is a polite form).

9. *Panini* = rolls. *Panino imbottito* = sandwich (stuffed roll).

10. *C'è del burro?* = Literally, have you of the butter? *del* = contraction of *di* and *il*

13. *Un uovo* = an egg. *Uova* = eggs. (Note the irregular plural.) *Uova alla cocca* = soft-boiled eggs ("in the shell"). *Uova sode* = hard-boiled eggs. *Uova strapazzate* = scrambled eggs.

14. *Tenga:* imperative of *tenere* (polite form). *Il resto* = the rest, the change (as a tip).

QUIZ 34

1. _____ (We would like) *fare colazione*.
   a. *Vorremmo*
   b. *Mangiare*
   c. *Appetito*
2. _____ (Is there) *del burro?*
   a. *Servire*
   b. *C'è*
   c. *Potrebbe?*
3. *Mi dia lo* _____ (same).
   a. *molto*
   b. *stesso*
   c. *spero*
4. *Chi vuole* _____ (eat)?
   a. *servire*
   b. *poco*
   c. *mangiare*
5. *Io mangio molto* _____ (little).
   a. *vado*
   b. *questo*
   c. *poco*
6. *Per favore* _____ (bring me) *un tovagliolo*.
   a. *costume*
   b. *mi porti*
   c. *dirà*
7. _____ (Then) *ci porti il conto*.
   a. *Favore*
   b. *Forchetta*
   c. *Poi*

ANSWERS
1—a; 2—b; 3—b; 4—c; 5—c; 6—b; 7—c.

B. A SAMPLE MENU

LISTA	MENU
Antipasto	Hors d'oeuvres
Minestrone	Vegetable soup
Passato di piselli	Pea soup
Frittata al prosciutto	Ham omelet
Pollo arrosto (pollo alla diavola)	Roast chicken (devil-style chicken)
Abbacchio (alla romana)	Roast lamb (Roman style)
Bistecca con patate fritte	Steak with French fried potatoes
Insalata verde con pomodori	Green salad with tomatoes
Formaggio e frutta	Cheese and fruit
Caffè	Coffee

LESSON 36

A. APARTMENT HUNTING

1. **Sono venuta a vedere l'appartamento.**
   I've come to see the apartment.

2. **Quale? Quale dei due?**
   Which one? Which of the two?

3. **Quello che è da affittare.**
   The one that is for rent.

4. **Ce ne sono due.**
   There are two.

5. **Me li può descrivere?**
   Can you describe them?

6. **Quello al quinto piano non è ammobiliato.**
   The one on the fifth floor is unfurnished.

7. **E quell'altro?**
   And the other one?

8. **L'altro al secondo piano è ammobiliato.**
   The one of the second floor is furnished.

9. **Quante camere ci sono?**
   How many rooms are there?

10. **Quello al quinto piano è di quattro camere, cucina
    e bagno.**
    The one on the fifth floor has four rooms, a kitchen and
    a bath.

11. **Dà sulla strada?**
    Does it face the street?

12. **No, sul cortile.**
    No, the courtyard.

13. **E quello al secondo piano?**
    And the one on the second floor?

14. **Quello al secondo piano ha una camera da letto, un
    salotto e una camera da pranzo.**
    The one on the third floor has a bedroom, a living
    room, and a dining room.

15. **Dà anche sul cortile?**
    Does it also face the courtyard?

16. **No, dà sulla strada.**
    No, it faces the street.

17. **Quanto è l'affitto?**
    How much is the rent?

18. **Il più grande costa quattromila euro al mese, più luce e gas.**
    The larger one is 4,000 euros a month, plus light and gas.

19. **E quello ammobiliato?**
    And the furnished one?

20. **Quello costa quattromilacinquecento euro al mese, tutto incluso.**
    That one costs 4,500 euros a month, everything included.

21. **Com'è ammobiliato? In che condizioni sono i mobili?**
    How is it furnished? In what condition is the furniture?

22. **I mobili sono moderni e sono in ottime condizioni.**
    It's modern furniture and it's in excellent condition.

23. **La biancheria e i piatti sono inclusi?**
    Are linen and silverware (dishes) included?

24. **Troverà tutto quello che Le occorre, perfino una batteria da cucina completa.**
    You'll find everything you need, even a complete set of kitchen utensils.

25. **Bisogna firmare un contratto lungo?**
    Do you have to sign a long lease?

26. **Per questo dovrà vedere l'amministratore.**
You'll have to see the rental agent for that.

27. **Quali sono le condizioni?**
What are the terms?

28. **Un mese anticipato e uno di deposito.**
One month's rent in advance and another month's rent as a deposit.

29. **È tutto?**
Is that all?

30. **Naturalmente, dovrà dare le Sue referenze.**
Of course you'll have to give references.

31. **A proposito, c'è l'ascensore?**
By the way, is there an elevator?

32. **No, non c'è ascensore.**
No, there is no elevator.

33. **Che peccato!**
That's too bad!

34. **A parte questo, la casa è molto moderna.**
Aside from that, the house is very modern.

35. **Che cosa vuol dire?**
What do you mean?

36. **C'è l'aria condizionata centrale.**
There's central air conditioning.

37. **C'è una lavanderia?**
Are there any laundry facilities?

38. **Naturalmente. E le camere da bagno sono state rimodernate di recente.**
Of course. And the bathrooms were recently remodeled.

39. **Si possono vedere gli appartamenti?**
Is it possible to see the apartments?

40. **Soltanto la mattina.**
Only in the morning.

41. **Va bene. Verrò domani mattina. Molte grazie.**
Very well. I'll come tomorrow morning. Thanks a lot.

42. **Di nulla. S'immagini. Felice di poterLa servire.**
Not at all. Don't mention it. Glad to be able to help you.

NOTES

1. *A* = in order to.

4. *Ce* is used instead of *ci*, because *ci, mi, ti, vi*, become *ce, me, te, ve* before *ne*.

5. *Me li:* as in 4.

9. *Ci sono* = there are.

11. Idiomatic expression. *Dare* = to give, but *dare su* = to face.

13. The first floor in Italy is called *pianterreno;* what we call the "second floor" in America is the *primo piano* in Italy.

21. *Il mobile* = piece of furniture. *I mobili* = the furniture *(pl.)*. *La mobilia, il mobilio* = furniture *(sing.)*

22. *Ottime:* superlative of *buone (fem. pl.).*

23. *I piatti* includes dishes and silverware. *Il piatto da portata* = the serving dish. *L' argenteria* = the silverware.

26. *L' amministratore* = the manager.

30. Note article in front of *sue (possessive).*

31. The definite article is often used in Italian where the indefinite is used in English.

33. *Che peccato!* = What a sin!

35. *Vuol:* the final *e (vuole)* of verb forms is often dropped in speaking.

38. *sono state rimodernate* = have been remodeled.

42. *S' immagini* = imagine. A polite way to express "Don't mention it." Also: *Ma le pare.*

QUIZ 35

1. _____ (I've come) *a vedere l' appartamento.*
   - a. *Sono venuta/-o*
   - b. *Sono*
   - c. *Voglio*
2. *Quello* _____ (for) *affittare.*
   - a. *in*
   - b. *per*
   - c. *da*
3. _____ (There are) *due.*
   - a. *C' è*
   - b. *Ce ne sono*
   - c. *Sono*

4. È _____ (without) *mobili.*
   a. *con*
   b. *senza*
   c. *tra*

5. _____ (How much) *è l'affitto?*
   a. *Quando*
   b. *Quanto*
   c. *Troppo*

6. _____ (Does it face) *sulla strada?*
   a. *Guarda*
   b. *Faccia*
   c. *Dà*

7. *Dà* _____ (also) *sul giardino?*
   a. *altro*
   b. *anche*
   c. *poi*

8. _____ (It costs) *un milione ottocentomila lire.*
   a. *Costa*
   b. *Quanto*
   c. *Viene*

9. *Bisogna* _____ (sign) *un contratto?*
   a. *scrivere*
   b. *segnare*
   c. *firmare*

10. *La casa è* _____ (very) *moderna.*
   a. *molto*
   b. *tanto*
   c. *male*

ANSWERS

1—a; 2—c; 3—b; 4—b; 5—b; 6—c; 7—b; 8—a; 9—c; 10—a.

SUPPLEMENTAL VOCABULARY 16: IN THE KITCHEN

refrigerator	*il frigorifero, il frigo*
(kitchen) sink	*il lavandino*
counter	*il piano*
stove	*la cucina elettrica/a gas*
oven	*il forno*
microwave	*il forno a microonde*
cupboard	*la credenza*
drawer	*il cassetto*
plate	*il piatto*
cup	*la tazza*
bowl	*la scodella* (small), *la ciotola, la terrina* (bigger)
glass	*il bicchiere*
spoon	*il cucchiaio*
knife	*il coltello*
can	*la lattina*
box	*la scatola*
bottle	*la bottiglia*
carton	*la scatola*
coffee maker	*la caffettiera* (small), *la macchina del caffè* (in a bar)
tea kettle	*il bollitore*
blender	*il frullatore*
iron	*il ferro da stiro*
ironing board	*l'asse da stiro*
broom	*la scopa*
dishwasher	*la lavapiatti, la lavastoviglie*
washing machine	*la lavatrice, la lavabiancheria*
dryer	*l'essicatrice*
to cook	*cucinare*
to do the dishes	*lavare i piatti*

to do the laundry	*fare la lavanderia, fare il bucato*
dishwashing detergent	*il detersivo per i piatti*
laundry detergent	*il detersivo per il bucato*
bleach	*la candeggina*
clean/dirty	*pulito/sporco*

SUPPLEMENTAL VOCABULARY 17: IN THE BATHROOM

toilet	*il water* (pronounced: *vater*)
sink (wash basin)	*il lavandino, il lavabo*
bath tub	*la vasca (da bagno)*
shower	*la doccia*
mirror	*lo specchio*
medicine cabinet	*l'armadietto*
towel	*l'asciugamano*
toilet paper	*la carta igienica*
shampoo	*lo shampo* (pronounced: *sciampo*)
soap	*la saponetta*
bath gel	*il bagnoschiuma, il docciaschiuma*
shaving cream	*la crema da barba*
razor	*il rasoio*
to wash onself	*lavarsi*
to take a shower/bath	*farsi il bagno/la doccia*
to shave	*farsi la barba, radersi*
cologne	*la colonia, il profumo*
perfume	*il profumo*
deodorant	*il deodorante*
bandage	*la benda, il cerotto*
powder	*il borotalco*

B. To Have: *AVERE*

io ho	I have
tu hai	you have
lui, lei, Lei ha	he, she has, you have
noi abbiamo	we have
voi avete	you have
loro hanno	they have

> *a.* *Avere* is also used in place of the English verb "to be" when talking about hunger, thirst, and other temporary conditions or feelings. *Avere* means "to have" in the sense of "to possess."

Ho questo.	I have this. I've got this.
Non ho nulla.	I don't have anything.
Ce l'ha Lei?	Do you have it?
Non ce l'ho.	I don't have it.
Ho tempo.	I have time.
Non ho denaro.	I don't have any money.
Non ho tempo.	I don't have any time.
Lui non ha amici.	He doesn't have any friends.
Ho fame.	I'm hungry.
Ho sete.	I'm thirsty.
Ho sonno.	I'm sleepy.
Ho freddo.	I'm cold.
Ho caldo.	I'm hot.
Ho ragione.	I'm right.
Lui non ha ragione.	He is not right.
Loro non hanno ragione.	They're wrong.
Ha degli amici a Roma?	Do you have (any) friends in Rome?
Io non ho amici a Roma.	I don't have any friends in Rome.
Ha una sigaretta?	Do you have a cigarette? *(pol.)*
Io non ho sigarette.	I don't have any cigarettes.

Ha un fiammifero?	Do you have a light (a match)? (*pol.*)
Non ho fiammiferi.	I don't have any matches.
Ho vent'anni.	I'm twenty.
Ho mal di testa.	I have a headache.
Ho mal di denti.	I have a toothache.
Che cosa hai?	What's the matter with you?
Non ho nulla.	Nothing's the matter with me.
Quanto denaro ha?	How much money do you have?
Io non ho denaro (affatto).	I don't have any money (at all).
Ho molto da fare.	I have a lot to do.

    b. Do I have it?

Ce l'ho io?	Do I have it?
Ce l'hai tu?	Do you have it? (*fam.*)
Ce l'ha Lei?	Do you have it? (*pol.*)
Ce l'ha lui?	Does he have it?
Ce l'abbiamo noi?	Do we have it?
Ce l'avete voi?	Do you have it? (*plural*)
Ce l'hanno loro?	Do they have it?

    c. Don't I have it?

Non ce l'ho (*lo ho*) **io?**	Don't I have it?
Non ce l'hai tu?	Don't you have it? (*fam.*)
Non ce l'ha Lei?	Don't you have it? (*pol.*)
Non ce l'ha lei?	Doesn't she have it?
Non ce l'abbiamo noi?	Don't we have it?
Non ce l'avete voi?	Don't you have it? (*pl.*)
Non ce l'hanno loro?	Don't they have it?

QUIZ 36

1. *Non ho denaro.*	a. I have a headache.
2. *Non ho nulla.*	b. Don't you have it?

3. *Lui non ha ragione.*	c. I don't have it.
4. *Ho sonno.*	d. I'm cold.
5. *Ce l' ha lui?*	e. I'm hot.
6. *Non ce l' ho.*	f. I don't have any money.
7. *Ho fame.*	g. Does he have it?
8. *Ho freddo.*	h. He's not right.
9. *Ho vent' anni.*	i. I'm thirsty.
10. *Non ce l' ha Lei?*	j. I have a lot to do.
11. *Io devo andare.*	k. I don't have anything.
12. *Ho caldo.*	l. I'm sleepy.
13. *Ho sete.*	m. I'm hungry.
14. *Ho mal di testa.*	n. I have to go.
15. *Ho molto da fare.*	o. I'm twenty years old.

ANSWERS

1—f; 2—k; 3—h; 4—l; 5—g; 6—c; 7—m; 8—d; 9—o;
10—b; 11—n; 12—e; 13—i; 14—a; 15—j.

LESSON 37

A. COULD YOU GIVE ME SOME INFORMATION?

1. **Mi scusi.**
   Pardon me. *(pol.)*

2. **In che cosa posso servirLa?**
   What can I do for you?/How can I help you?

3. **Mi potrebbe dare alcune informazioni?**
   Could you give me some information?

4. **Con molto piacere.**
   Gladly. (With much pleasure.)

5. **Io non conosco questa città e non mi posso orientare.**
   I don't know this city, and I can't find my way around.

6. **Bene, è abbastanza semplice.**
   Well, it's quite simple.

7. **Come vede, io sono straniera.**
   As you see, I'm a foreigner (here).

8. **In questo caso Le mostrerò la città.**
   In that case I'll show you the town.

9. **La ringrazierò moltissimo. Lo apprezzerò molto.**
   I'd be very grateful to you. I'd appreciate that a lot.

10. **Vede quel gran palazzo all'angolo?**
    Do you see that large building on the corner?

11. **Quello con la bandiera?**
    The one with the flag?

12. **Esattamente. Quello è la Posta Centrale.**
    Exactly. That's the Main Post Office.

    Di fronte dall'altro lato della strada . . .
    Opposite, on the other side of the street . . .

13. **Dove?**
    Where?

14. **Da quella parte. Vede quell'altro palazzo con gli archi?**
    Over there. Do you see that other building with arches?

15. **Oh, sì, adesso lo vedo.**
    Oh, yes, now I see it.

16. **Quella è la Galleria Colonna.**
That's the Colonna Gallery.

17. **La vedo. . . . A proposito, qual'è il nome di questa piazza?**
I see it. . . . By the way, what's the name of this square?

18. **Piazza San Silvestro.**
Saint Sylvester Square.

19. **Dov'è la Questura?**
Where is the Police Station?

20. **In fondo a quella strada, a destra.**
At the end of the street, to the right.

21. **E se non la trovo?**
What if I miss it (if I don't find it)?

22. **Non si preoccupi.**
Don't worry. *(pol.)*

È un gran palazzo grigio, con due guardie di fronte all'entrata.
It's a big, gray building with two guards in front of the entrance.
Vede quel negozio?
You see that store?

23. **Quale negozio? Quello a sinistra?**
Which store? The one on the left?

24. **Esattamente. Quello che ha quel grosso globo di vetro verde in vetrina.**
Right. The one with the large green glass globe in the window.

25. **È una barbieria?**
It's a barbershop?

26. **No, è una farmacia.**
No, it's a pharmacy.

Al lato del negozio c'è la casa del dottore.
The doctor lives right next door. (Next to the store is
the doctor's house.)

Il suo nome è sulla porta.
His name is on the door.

27. **Ha l'ufficio nella stessa casa in cui abita?**
Does he have his office there as well? (Does he have
his office in the same house in which he lives?)

28. **Sì, ma tutte le mattine va all'ospedale.**
Yes, but he spends every morning at the hospital.

29. **Dov'è l'ospedale?**
Where is the hospital?

30. **Per raggiungere l'ospedale, Lei deve camminare
per Corso Umberto, verso Piazza del Popolo.**
To reach the hospital, you must take the Umberto
Corso (Avenue) toward Popolo Square.

**Alla penultima strada a sinistra si trova Via San
Giacomo, e l'Ospedale San Giacomo è là.**
A block before reaching the Square, you will come to
Saint Giacomo (James) Street on the left, and the Saint
Giacomo hospital is there.

31. **Come posso ritornare al mio albergo?**
How can I get back to my hotel?

32. **Vada per questa strada. Lo vede là, dopo il ...**
    Go this way. You see it there, next to the ...

33. **... cinema? Non è così?**
    ... movies? Right? (Isn't it so?)

34. **Esatto.**
    Yes. (Exactly.)

35. **Ora ho capito.**
    Now I understand.

36. **Perchè non si compra una guida?**
    Why don't you buy yourself a guidebook?

37. **Non è una cattiva idea. Dove posso comprarla?**
    That's not a bad idea. Where can I buy one?

38. **Alla stazione, oppure in qualsiasi edicola.**
    At the train station, or at any newsstand.

39. **È lontana da qui la stazione?**
    Is the station far from here?

40. **La stazione si trova in Piazza Cinquecento.**
    The station is in Cinquecento (Five Hundred) Square.

41. **Dove si trova un edicola qui vicino?**
    Where's there a newsstand near here?

42. **Ce n'è una all'angolo.**
    There's one on the corner.

43. **La ringrazio molto.**
    Thank you very much. (I thank you very much.)

44. **Non c'è di che.**
Not at all.

Sono molto lieto di esserLe stato utile.
I'm very glad to have been of help to you. (I'm very glad to have been useful to you.)

45. **Sono stata molto fortunata di averLa incontrata.**
I was certainly lucky to meet you.

Lei conosce questa città molto bene.
You really know this town very well.

46. **Non si sorprenda. Io sono il Sindaco.**
It's not surprising. I'm the mayor.

NOTES

3. *Potrebbe:* conditional of *potere.*

6. *Abbastanza* = enough.

9. *Apprezzerò:* future of *apprezzare.*

10. *Gran:* abbreviated form of *grande.*

12. *La posta centrale* = main post office. *La posta* = the mail.

14. *Palazzo* = building; also *edificio. Il palazzo* can also be "a palace."

24. In Italy, pharmacies usually have a green globe, or a big vase, in the window.

25. *La barbieria* = the barber shop; *un barbiere* = a barber; can also be called *parrucchiere.*

30. *La penultima strada* = the street before the last. In Italy, people count by streets, not by blocks. There is actually

no real word for block, although *isolato* is sometimes used. *Caseggiato* is a group of buildings that might sometimes correspond to an American block.

33. *Cinema* is really the "movie theater." The movie (film) is called *la pellicola*, or *il film*.

35. *Ho capito* = I understood. This is the past tense, but this expression is often used instead of *capisco* with the same meaning.

37. *Cattiva* = bad, meaning literally "ugly." *Brutto* is also often used with the meaning of "bad." *Che brutta idea!* = What a bad idea!

44. *Non c'è di che.* (There is nothing about it . . . You are welcome.) A polite formula to use in answer to *grazie* (thank you). Another common expression is *prego*. *Sono molto lieto(a) di esserle stato(a) utile.* (I am very glad to have been of help to you.) A polite expression.

46. *Non si sorprenda.* = Literally, don't surprise yourself.

QUIZ 37

1. *È molto* _____ (simple).
   a. *poco*
   b. *semplice*
   c. *città*

2. *Le farò vedere la* _____ (city).
   a. *caso*
   b. *città*
   c. *orientare*

3. *Questo grande palazzo all'* _____ (corner).
   a. *angolo*
   b. *via*
   c. *ufficio postale*

4. *Questo è l'* _____ (post office).
   a. *via*
   b. *ufficio postale*
   c. *altro*

5. *Vede questo* _____ (store)?
   a. *destra*
   b. *negozio*
   c. *barbiere*

6. *Nella casa vicina c'è un* _____ (doctor).
   a. *dottore*
   b. *farmacia*
   c. *nome*

7. *Il suo nome è sulla* _____ (door).
   a. *stesso*
   b. *porta*
   c. *clinica*

8. *Ha l'ufficio nella stessa* _____ (house) *in cui vive?*
   a. *dopo*
   b. *lato*
   c. *casa*

9. *Un poco* _____ (before) *di arrivare alla strada principale.*
   a. *dopo*
   b. *prima*
   c. *passata*

10. *Dove posso* _____ (buy) *questo?*
    a. *comprare*
    b. *guida*
    c. *stazione*

ANSWERS

1—b; 2—b; 3—a; 4—b; 5—b; 6—a; 7—b; 8—c; 9—b;
10—a.

SUPPLEMENTAL VOCABULARY 18: ENTERTAINMENT

movie/film	*film*
to go to the movies	*andare al cinema*
to see a movie	*vedere un film*
theater	*il cinema* (movies), *il teatro* (plays)
to see a play	*vedere uno spettacolo*
opera	*l' opera*
concert	*il concerto*
club	*il club* (pronounced: *cleb*)
circus	*il circo*
ticket	*il biglietto*
museum	*il museo*
gallery	*la galleria*
painting	*il quadro*
sculpture	*la scultura*
television program	*la trasmissione televisiva*
to watch television	*guardare la tivù/la tele/la televisione*
comedy	*la commedia*
documentary	*il documentario*
dram	*il dramma*
book	*il libro*
magazine	*la rivista*
to read a book	*leggere un libro*
to read a magazine	*leggere una rivista*
to listen to music	*ascoltare la musica*
song	*la canzone*
band	*il gruppo*
the news	*le notizie, il telegiornale/il TG (ti-gi)* (on TV), *il giornale radio* (on the radio)
talk show	*talk show*

to flip channels	*cambiare canale*
to have fun	*divertirsi*
to be bored	*annoiarsi*
funny	*divertente*
interesting	*interessante*
exciting	*stimolante*
scary	*fa paura, spaventevole*
party	*la festa*
restaurant	*il ristorante*
concert	*il concerto*
opera	*l'opera* (f.)
to go to a party	*andare a una festa*
to have a party	*dare una festa*
to dance	*ballare*

LESSON 38

A. A CHANCE MEETING

1. Antonio: **Ester, come stai?**
   Esther, how are you?

   Come stanno Sandro e Silvana?
   How are Sandro and Silvana?

2. Ester: **Bene, e tu e Lina come state? E i ragazzi?**
   Fine. And how are you and Lina? And the children?

3. A: **Benissimo. Io e Lina lavoriamo.**
   Very well. Lina and I work.

   I ragazzi vanno a scuola.
   The children go to school.

4. E: **Giovanni va già all'università, vero?**
John's already in college, right?

5. A: **Sì, fa il primo anno.**
Yes, he's in his first year.

   Studia a Roma.
   He's studying in Rome.

   Deve sempre studiare—non lo vediamo mai.
   He always has to study—we never see him.

6. E: **Anche Silvana studia sempre, legge sempre, scrive sempre.**
Silvana is also always studying, always reading, always writing.

   L'ultimo anno di liceo è sempre difficile.
   The last year of *liceo* is always difficult.

7. A: **Sai, anch'io seguo un corso serale, un corso d'inglese.**
You know, I'm taking a night class, too, an English class.

8. E: **Bravo!**
Bravo!

   Giochi ancora a tennis con gli amici?
   Do you still play tennis with your friends?

9. A: **No, non ho più tempo.**
No, I don't have the time anymore.

NOTES

2. The *tu (fam.)* pronoun and form of the verb is used because two friends are speaking.

3. Note the usage of the suffix *-issimo* to mean "very," e.g., *buonissimo* = very good, *dolcissimo* = very sweet. Also: *carissimo/a* = dearest.

5. *Non lo vediamo mai.* An example of the double negation often used in Italian.

6. Note that *sempre* (always) usually follows the verb. A *liceo* is a secondary school that focuses on the humanities or science.

7. *Seguire un corso* = to take (literally "to follow") a class.

8. *Ancora* = still; *non ancora* = not yet; *già* = already.

B. AT THE TOBACCO SHOP

1. Mark: **Un pacchetto di Nazionali, per favore.**
   A pack of *Nazionali*, please.

2. Tobacconist: **Con filtro o senza filtro?**
   Filtered or nonfiltered?

3. M: **Con filtro.**
   Filtered.

4. T: **Altro?**
   Anything else?

5. M: **Sì, una scatola di cerini ... Qui si vendono biglietti per l'autobus?**
   Yes, a box of matches ... Do you sell bus tickets here?

6. T: **Quanti ne vuole?**
   How many (of them) would you like?

7. M: **Soltanto uno. Dove si può trovare della carta da lettere?**
   Only one. Where can I find some writing paper?

8. T: **Anche qui si vende carta da lettere.**
   We sell writing paper here as well.

9. M: **Davvero?**
   Really?

10. T: **Sì, qui in Italia dai tabaccai si vende un po' di tutto.**
    Yes, here in Italy we sell a little bit of everything in tobacco shops.

    Si possono comprare sigarette, fiammiferi, accendini, francobolli, cartoline . . .
    You can buy cigarettes, matches, lighters, stamps, postcards . . .

    Articoli da regalo come profumi, giocattoli . . .
    Gift items like perfumes, toys . . .

11. M: **Si vendono anche rullini?**
    Do you also sell film?

12. T: **Sì.**
    Yes.

13. M: **Allora, della carta da lettere e un rullino a colori da ventiquattro pose.**
    So, some writing paper and a roll of 24-exposure color film.

14. T: **Ecco a Lei.**
    Here you go.

15. M: **Un'ultima cosa ... Dove si può trovare un tele-
    fono pubblico?**
    One last thing ... Where can I find a pay phone?

16. T: **Il telefono è proprio qui.**
    The phone is right here.

    Le servono dei gettoni o una carta telefonica?
    Do you need tokens or a phone card?

NOTES

5. *Si* plus the *lei* or *loro* form of a word is used in impersonal expressions where the subject is the general
   "one," "we," "they," "people," or "you." For example:
   Qui si parla italiano. They/People speak Italian here.

7. The preposition *da* is often used to specify the purpose
   of an object: *carta da lettere* = paper for writing.

10. *Un po' di tutto* = a little bit of everything. *Po'* is short
    for *poco*, "little," "few."

13. The preposition *di* is used to express "some." Note
    the contracted forms: *di + il = del; di + la = della;
    di + i = dei; di + le = delle.*

16. *Le servono dei gettoni* = Are tokens of use to you?
    Another way to express "to need" is *avere bisogno di:
    Ha bisogno di gettoni* = Do you need tokens?

QUIZ 38

1. _____ (How) *stai?*
   a. *Qui*
   b. *Dove*
   c. *Come*

2. *Giovanni* _____ (is going) *già all' università.*
   a. *fa*
   b. *va*
   c. *vanno*

3. *Giovanni* _____ (is in) *il primo anno.*
   a. *fa*
   b. *va*
   c. *vanno*

4. *Non lo vediamo* _____ (never).
   a. *sempre*
   b. *mai*
   c. *più*

5. *L'ultimo anno di liceo è* _____ (always) *difficile.*
   a. *sempre*
   b. *mai*
   c. *più*

6. *Anch'io* _____ (am taking) *un corso d'inglese.*
   a. *sto*
   b. *vado*
   c. *seguo*

7. _____ (How many) *ne vuole?*
   a. *Quanti*
   b. *Come*
   c. *Quando*

8. *Qui* _____ (they sell) *carta da lettere.*
   a. *vende*
   b. *soltanto*
   c. *si vende*

9. *Dai* _____ (tobacco shops) *si vende un po' di tutto.*
   a. *sigarette*
   b. *tabaccai*
   c. *fiammiferi*

10. *Dove si può trovare un* _____ (pay phone)?
   a. *telefono pubblico*
   b. *gettoni*
   c. *carta telefonica*

ANSWERS

1—c; 2—b; 3—a; 4—b; 5—a; 6—c; 7—a; 8—c; 9—b;
10—a.

LESSON 39

A. SOME IMPORTANT IRREGULAR VERBS

1. *Potere* = to be able

PRESENT	PRESENT PERFECT	FUTURE	PAST PARTICIPLE
io posso	io ho potuto	io potrò	potuto
tu puoi	tu hai potuto	tu potrai	
lui può	lui ha potuto	lui potrà	
lei può	lei ha potuto	lei potrà	
noi possiamo	noi abbiamo potuto	noi potremo	
voi potete	voi avete potuto	voi potrete	
Loro possono	Loro hanno potuto	Loro potranno	
loro possono	loro hanno potuto	loro potranno	

Posso?	May I? Can I?
Dove posso mandare un facsìmile/un fax?	Where can I send a fax?
Potrai venire questa sera?	Will you be able to come tonight?
Posso parlare con lui?	May I speak with him?

2. *Dovere* = to have to

| | PRESENT | | PAST |
PRESENT	PERFECT	FUTURE	PARTICIPLE
io devo	io ho dovuto	io dovrò	dovuto
tu devi	tu hai dovuto	tu dovrai	
lui deve	lui ha dovuto	lui dovrà	
noi dobbiamo	noi abbiamo dovuto	noi dovremo	
voi dovete	voi avete dovuto	voi dovrete	
loro devono	loro hanno dovuto	loro dovranno	

Devo farlo.	I must do it.
Io devo andare.	I have to leave.
Io ti devo cinque dollari.	I owe you five dollars.
Dovrei *(conditional)* **andarci.**	I should go there.

3. *Volere* = to want

| | PRESENT | | PAST |
PRESENT	PERFECT	FUTURE	PARTICIPLE
io voglio	io ho voluto	io vorrò	voluto
tu vuoi	tu hai voluto	tu vorrai	
lui vuole	lui ha voluto	lui vorrà	
noi vogliamo	noi abbiamo voluto	noi vorremo	

| voi volete | voi avete voluto | voi vorrete |
| loro vogliono | loro hanno voluto | loro vorranno |

Voler bene a qualcuno.	To like someone.
Voglio farlo.	I want to do it.
Vorrei (*conditional*) **finire.**	I would like to finish.

4. *Sapere* = to know

PRESENT	PRESENT PERFECT	FUTURE	PAST PARTICIPLE
io so	**io ho saputo**	**io saprò**	**saputo**
tu sai	**tu hai saputo**	**tu saprai**	
lui sa	**lui ha saputo**	**lui saprà**	
noi sappiamo	**noi abbiamo saputo**	**noi sapremo**	
voi sapete	**voi avete saputo**	**voi saprete**	
loro sanno	**loro hanno saputo**	**loro sapranno**	

Lo so che è vero.	I know it's true.
Hai saputo la notizia?	Did you hear the news?
Loro lo sapranno in tempo.	They'll find out in time.

5. *Andare* = to go

PRESENT	PRESENT PERFECT	FUTURE	PAST PARTICIPLE
io vado	**io sono andato**(-*a*)	**io andrò**	**andato**
tu vai	**tu sei andato**(-*a*)	**tu andrai**	

lui va	lui è andato	lui andrà
noi andiamo	noi siamo andati(-e)	noi andremo
voi andate	voi siete andati(-e)	voi andrete
loro vanno	loro sono andati(-e)	loro andranno

Sono andato a piedi.	I walked. (I went on foot.)
Andremo insieme.	We'll go together.
Vada presto! *(pol. imperative)*	Go quickly!
Andiamo!	Let's go!

6. *Venire* = to come

	PRESENT		PAST
PRESENT	PERFECT	FUTURE	PARTICIPLE
io vengo	io sono venuto(-a)	io verrò	venuto
tu vieni	tu sei venuto(-a)	tu verrai	
lui viene	lui è venuto	lui verrà	
noi veniamo	noi siamo venuti(-e)	noi verremo	
voi venite	voi siete venuti(-e)	voi verrete	
loro vengono	loro sono venuti(-e)	loro verranno	

Vieni con me, non è vero?	You're coming with me, aren't you?
Viene sempre da me.	He always comes to my house.
Quando verrà lei?	When will she come?
Vengono spesso in città.	They often come to the city.
Venga *(imperative)* **domani verso le tre.**	Come tomorrow at about three.

LESSON 40

A. FUN IN ITALIAN

UN'OTTIMISTA

Il capo di un'importante casa commerciale, leggendo una richiesta di lavoro, si meraviglia moltissimo nel notare che il richiedente, pur non avendo esperienza, domanda uno stipendio eccessivo.

-Non Le sembra di richiedere uno stipendio troppo alto, considerando la Sua poca esperienza in merito?

-Tutt'altro, assumere un lavoro del quale non si sa assolutamente nulla, è cosa molto più difficile, e dovrebbe essere pagata molto meglio.

AN OPTIMIST

The head of an important firm, looking at a job application, is astonished when he notices that the applicant, though lacking experience, is asking for a high salary.

"Doesn't it seem to you that you are asking for an excessive salary, considering the little experience you have?"

"On the contrary, work performed by one who knows nothing about it is more difficult and should be better paid."

NOTES

1. *Si meraviglia moltissimo* = is very much amazed. *Meravigliarsi:* to wonder, to be astonished, to be surprised.

2. *Nel* is a contraction for *in* and *il*.

3. *Pur* = although. (Always followed by the participle.)

4. *Le sembra* = It seems to you. *Mi sembra* = It seems to me. *Ci sembra* = It seems to us.

5. *tutt' altro* = everything else, on the contrary.

6. *dovrebbe:* conditional of *dovere (dovrebbe* = it should be).

UNA PERDITA DI POCA IMPORTANZA

CLIENTE: Signora, per favore, mi dia una copia del "Messaggero." Non ho spiccioli. Può cambiarmi questi cinque euro?
GIORNALAIA: Può pagarmi domani.
CLIENTE: E se morissi questa notte?
GIORNALAIA: Oh, non sarebbe davvero una grande perdita.

A MINOR LOSS

CUSTOMER: Miss, could you please give me a copy of the *Messenger?* I don't have any change. Could you change this bill of five euros for me?
NEWSSTAND ATTENDANT: You can pay for it tomorrow.
CUSTOMER: What if I die tonight?
ATTENDANT: Oh, it wouldn't be a very great loss.

NOTES

1. *Spiccioli* = change (money).

2. *E se morissi:* if I were to die (past subjunctive of *morire*).

3. *Sarebbe:* conditional of "to be" (It would [not] be).

UNA LEZIONE DI ETICHETTA

Pietro e Giovanni vanno a mangiare in un ristorante. Entrambi ordinano una bistecca. Il cameriere li serve poco dopo. Pietro afferra subito la bistecca più grande. Giovanni, seccato, gli dice:

-Come sei maleducato! Ti servi per primo e ti prendi anche il pezzo più grande.

Pietro gli risponde:

-Se tu fossi stato al mio posto, quale pezzo avresti scelto?

-Il più piccolo, naturalmente.

-E allora, perchè ti lamenti?

A LESSON IN ETIQUETTE

Peter and John go to a restaurant to eat. They both order steak. The waiter brings the steaks to them shortly afterward. Peter grabs the larger steak. John says to him angrily:

"What bad manners you have! You helped yourself first and you took the larger piece."

Pietro answers:

"If you had been in my place, which piece would you have taken?

"The smaller, of course."

"Then what are you complaining about? You have it, don't you?"

NOTES

1. *Entrambi* = both of them; also *tutti e due*.

3. *Se tu fossi stato* = if you had been. (The pluperfect subjunctive is used in this case to indicate a condition contrary to fact.)

4. *Avresti scelto:* past conditional of *scegliere;* expresses the second part of the conditional sentence. *Se io fossi stato in quel ristorante, avrei ordinato pollo arrosto.* If I had been in that restaurant, I would have ordered roast chicken.

5. *Ti lamenti* = you lament yourself. *Lamentarsi:* reflexive verb meaning "to lament," "to complain."

B. IMPORTANT SIGNS

Signori or *Uomini*	Men
Signore or *Donne*	Women
Gabinetto	Toilet
Chiuso	Closed
Aperto	Open
Proibito fumare	No Smoking
Vietato fumare	No Smoking
Vietato l'ingresso	No Admittance
Bussare	Knock
Suonare il campanello	Ring
Strada privata	Private Street
Per informazioni rivolgersi qui	Inquire Within
Alt! Stop! Fermo!	Stop!
Via libera!	Go!
Attenzione!	Look Out!
Pericolo	Danger
Rallentare	Go Slow
Svolta obbligata	Detour
Attenzione	Caution (Look Out)
Mantenere la destra	Keep to the Right
Ponte	Bridge
Divieto di sosta	No Parking
Ufficio controllo	Check Room
Cambio	Money Exchange
Informazioni	Information
Sala d'aspetto	Waiting Room
Vietato sporgersi (dalla finestra)	Don't Lean Out (of the window)
Treno merci	Freight Car
Binario ferroviario	Railroad Track
Direttissimo	Express
Accelerato (locale)	Local

Fermata	Stop (bus, streetcar, etc.)
Vietata l' affissione	Post No Bills
In riparazione	Under Repair
Entrata	Entrance
Uscita	Exit
Camere ammobiliate	Furnished Rooms
Appartamenti	Apartments
Pittura fresca	Wet Paint
Incrocio	Crossroads/Intersection
Macelleria	Butcher (Butcher's Shop)
Panificio	Bakery
Latteria	Dairy
Sartoria	Tailor Shop (also for women)
Calzoleria	Shoe Store
Barbiere	Barbershop (barber)
Salumeria	Grocer
Farmacia	Pharmacy, Drugstore
Pasticceria	Candy Store
Cartoleria	Stationery Store
Cassetta delle lettere	Mail Box
Buca delle lettere	Mail Box
Bar	Bar
Questura	Police Station
Vini	Wines
Distributore benzina	Gas Station
Libreria	Bookstore
Comune Municipo	City Hall
Bibite—Gelati	Drinks—Ice Cream
Acqua fredda	Cold Water
Acqua calda	Hot Water

QUIZ 39

1. *Entrata*   a. No Smoking
2. *Svolta obbligata*   b. Express

3. *Vietato sporgersi (dalla*   c. No Parking
   finestra)
4. *Chiuso*   d. Open
5. *Aperto*   e. Exit
6. *Vietato fumare*   f. Information
7. *Espresso*   g. Detour
8. *Divieto di sosta*   h. Entrance
9. *Uscita*   i. Closed
10. *Informazioni*   j. Don't Lean Out (of the
                                       window)

ANSWERS

1—h; 2—g; 3—j; 4—i; 5—d; 6—a; 7—b; 8—c; 9—e;
10—f.

FINAL QUIZ

1. _____ (Tell me) *dov'è la stazione.*
   a. *Mi permetta*
   b. *Mi dica*
   c. *Mi porti*
2. _____ (Can) *dirmi dov'è l'ufficio postale?*
   a. *Può*
   b. *Avere*
   c. *Costo*
3. *Dove* _____ (is) *un buon ristorante?*
   a. *fare*
   b. *c'è*
   c. *oggi*
4. _____ (Bring me) *un po' di pane.*
   a. *ConoscerLa*
   b. *Mi permetta*
   c. *Mi porti*
5. _____ (I need) *di sapone.*
   a. *Ho bisogno*
   b. *Avere*
   c. *Permette*

6. _____ (I would like) *un po' più di carne.*
    a. *Mi porti*
    b. *Mi manca*
    c. *Vorrei*

7. *La* _____ (I introduce) *alla mia amica.*
    a. *presento*
    b. *ho*
    c. *venga*

8. *Dov'* _____ (is) *il libro?*
    a. *è*
    b. *quello*
    c. *questo*

9. _____ (Please) *parli lentamente.*
    a. *La bontà*
    b. *Per piacere*
    c. *Il favore*

10. _____ (Do you understand) *l' italiano?*
    a. *Comprendo*
    b. *Parla*
    c. *Capisce*

11. _____ (Go) *là.*
    a. *Vada*
    b. *Parla*
    c. *Essere*

12. _____ (Come) *subito.*
    a. *Venga*
    b. *Vado*
    c. *Andiamo*

13. *Come si* _____ (call) *Lei?*
    a. *lavare*
    b. *chiama*
    c. *chiamano*

14. *Che giorno della* _____ (week) *è oggi?*
    a. *settimana*
    b. *mese*
    c. *anno*

15. *Che* _____ (time) *è?*
    a. *ora*
    b. *adesso*
    c. *ho*

16. *Non* _____ (I have) *sigarette.*
    a. *tempo*
    b. *ho*
    c. *avere*

17. _____ (Do you want) *della frutta?*
    a. *Potrebbe*
    b. *Ha lei*
    c. *Desidera*

18. _____ (Allow me) *di presentarLa al mio amico.*
    a. *Dare*
    b. *Mi permetta*
    c. *Mi porti*

19. _____ (I want) *scrivere una lettera.*
    a. *Desidera*
    b. *Voglio*
    c. *Mi permetta*

20. *Quanto* _____ (costs) *una telefonata a Milano?*
    a. *costa*
    b. *costare*
    c. *conto*

21. *Desideriamo fare* _____ (breakfast).
    a. *colazione*
    b. *cena*
    c. *pranzo*

22. *È l'* _____ (1:45).
    a. *una a trenta*
    b. *una e quarantacinque*
    c. *una e quindici*

23. *Venga* _____ (tomorrow morning).
    a. *ieri mattina*
    b. *domani mattina*
    c. *domani a mezzogiorno*

24. *In che* _____ (can I) *servirLa?*
    a. *può*
    b. *posso*
    c. *possono*
25. *Non* _____ (has) *importanza.*
    a. *avere*
    b. *ha*
    c. *avuto*

ANSWERS

1—b; 2—a; 3—b; 4—c; 5—a; 6—c; 7—a; 8—a; 9—a;
10—c; 11—a; 12—a; 13—b; 14—a; 15—a; 16—b; 17—c;
18—b; 19—b; 20—a; 21—a; 22—b; 23—b; 24—b; 25—b.

SUMMARY OF ITALIAN GRAMMAR

1. ALPHABET

LETTER	NAME	LETTER	NAME	LETTER	NAME
a	*a*	h	*acca*	q	*qu*
b	*bi*	i	*i*	r	*erre*
c	*ci*	l	*elle*	s	*esse*
d	*di*	m	*emme*	t	*ti*
e	*e*	n	*enne*	u	*u*
f	*effe*	o	*o*	v	*vu/vi*
g	*gi*	p	*pi*	z	*zeta*

2. PRONUNCIATION

SIMPLE VOWELS

a	as in *ah* or *father*
e	as in *day*, *ace*
i	as in *machine*, *police*
o	as in *no*, *note*
u	as in *rule*

VOWEL COMBINATIONS

ai	ai in *aisle*
au	ou in *out*
ei	ay-ee
eu	ay-oo
ia	ya in *yard*
ie	ye in *yes*
io	yo in *yoke*
iu	you
oi	oy in *boy*
ua	wah
ue	way
ui	oo-ee
uo	oo-oh

CONSONANTS

h	is never pronounced
ll	When two consonants occur in
mm	the middle of a word, they are both pronounced.
nn	Notice the difference between the following:
rr	*caro*, dear, *carro*, truck
ss	*casa*, house, *cassa*, case
	pala, shovel, *palla*, ball

1. *ci, ce* is pronounced like the English *ch* in *chair:*

cacciatore   hunter

2. *ch* before *e* and *i* is pronounced like the English *k* in *key:*

chitarra   guitar

3. *gi, ge* is pronounced like *j* in *jail:*

generoso   generous

4. *gh* before *e* and *i* is pronounced like the English *g* in *gate:*

ghirlanda   garland

5. *gli.* The closest English approximation is the combination *lli* as in *million:*

figlio   son   *paglia*   straw

6. *gn* is always pronounced as one letter, somewhat like the English *ni* in *onion* or *ny* in *canyon:*

segno   sign   *Spagna*   Spain

7. *sc* before *e* and *i* is pronounced like the English *sh* in *shoe:*

scendere   (to) descend   *sciroppo*   syrup

8. *sc* before *a, o,* and *u* is pronounced like the English *sk* in *sky:*

scuola   school   *scarpa*   shoe

3. STRESS

1. Words of two syllables are generally stressed on the first syllable, unless the other one bears an accent mark:

matita	pencil	*città*	city
penna	pen	*virtù*	virtue
meta	goal	*metà*	half

2. Words of more than two syllables are generally stressed either on the syllable before the last, or on the syllable before that:

ancora	more	*ancora*	anchor
dolore	grief	*amore*	love
scatola	box	*automobile*	car

4. USE OF THE DEFINITE ARTICLE

il, l' and *lo* (masc. sing.)   *la* and *l'* (fem. sing.)
i and *gli* (masc. pl.)   *le* (fem. pl.)

There are many instances in which Italian uses a definite article where no article is used in English:

Il tempo è denaro.	Time is money.
La vita è piena di guai.	Life is full of troubles.
I lupi sono feroci.	Wolves are ferocious.
I cani sono fedeli.	Dogs are faithful.
L'oro è un metallo prezioso.	Gold is a precious metal.
Il ferro è duro.	Iron is hard.
Gli affari sono affari.	Business is business.
La necessità non conosce legge.	Necessity knows no law.

Remember that in Italian you generally find the definite article in front of a possessive adjective or pronoun:

Il mio libro è nero, il tuo rosso. My book is black, yours red.

But with nouns indicating a family member in the singular, no article is used with the possessive adjective:

mio padre	my father
tuo fratello	your brother
nostro zio	our uncle

When *loro* (their or your) is used or when the relationship noun is modified, the definite article precedes the possessive:

la loro mamma	their mother
il mio padre generoso	my generous father

In expressions like the following, Italian uses the definite article:

Tre volte la settimana	Three times a week.
Due euro al kilo.	Two euros a kilo.

The definite article is used when talking about parts of the human body.

Il signore ha il naso lungo.	The gentleman has a long nose.

The definite article is always used with expressions of time:

Sono le due.	It is two o'clock.

With some geographical expressions:

L'Europa è un continente.	Europe is a continent.
La Toscana è bella.	Toscany is beautiful.

5. USE OF THE INDEFINITE ARTICLE

Un, uno, una, un'

Italian uses no indefinite article in cases like the following ones:

Io sono maestro.	I am a teacher.
Che donna!	What a woman!
mezzo chilo	half a kilo
cento uomini	a hundred men

6. THE PLURAL

There is no special plural form for:

1. Nouns with a written accent on the last vowel:

la città	the city
le città	the cities
il caffè	the coffee
i caffè	the coffees

2. Nouns ending in *i* in the singular, and almost all the nouns in *ie:*

il brindisi	the toast
i brindisi	the toasts
la crisi	the crisis
le crisi	the crises
la superficie	the surface
le superficie	the surfaces

3. Nouns ending in a consonant:

il bar	the bar
i bar	the bars
il computer	the computer
i computer	the computers

7. THE PARTITIVE

1. The partitive can be expressed in Italian in several ways:

a. With the preposition *di* + a form of the definite article *il, lo, la:*

Io mangio del pane.	I eat some (of the) bread.
Io mangio della carne.	I eat some meat.
Io prendo dello zucchero.	I take some sugar.
Io leggo dei libri.	I read some books.
Io scrivo degli esercizi.	I write some exercises.
Io compro delle sedie.	I buy some chairs.

b. By using *qualche* (only with singular nouns):

Io scrivo qualche lettera.	I write a few letters.
Io leggo qualche giornale.	I read a few (some) newspapers.

c. By using *alcuni, alcune* (only in the plural):

Io ho alcuni amici.	I have a few friends.
Io scrivo alcune poesie.	I write a few poems.

d. By using *un po' di:*

Io prendo un po' di zucchero.	I'll take some sugar.

2. In some cases, especially if the sentence is negative, Italian does not use any partitive at all:

Io non mangio cipolle.   I don't eat onions.

8. ADJECTIVES

1. Most singular adjectives end in *-o* for the masculine and *-a* for the feminine:

un caro amico   a dear friend *(masc.)*
una cara amica   a dear friend *(fem.)*

2. Most plural adjectives end in *-i* for the masculine and *-e* for the feminine:

cari amici   dear friends *(masc.)*
care amiche   dear friends *(fem.)*

3. Some singular adjectives end in *-e* in the masculine and in the feminine:

un uomo gentile   a kind man
una donna gentile   a kind woman

In the plural these same adjectives end in *i* in both the masculine and the feminine:

uomini gentili   kind men
donne gentili   kind women

9. POSITION OF THE ADJECTIVE

In general, adjectives follow the noun. Some common exceptions are: *buono* (good), *cattivo* (bad), *nuovo* (new), *bello* (beautiful), and *brutto* (ugly).

la musica italiana	Italian music
il libro nero	the black book
una brutta giornata	an awful day
un nuovo libro	a new book

Possessive adjectives, demonstrative adjectives, numerals, and indefinite adjectives generally precede the noun:

il mio amico	my friend
questo libro	this book
due penne	two pens
alcuni signori	a few men

10. COMPARISON

(così) . . . come	as . . . as
tanto . . . quanto	as much/as many . . . as
più . . . di or che	more . . . than
meno . . . di or che	fewer/less . . . than

Il mio appartamento è grande come il tuo.	My apartment is as large as yours.
Luigi legge tanto quanto Paola.	Luigi reads as much as Paola.

After *più* and *meno,* either *di* or *che* can be used, but if the comparison is between two adjectives, or if there is a preposition, only *che* can be used:

Franco è più studioso di Carlo.	Frank is more studious than Charles.
Franco è meno alto di Luca.	Carlo is less tall than Luca.
Giacomo è più studioso che intelligente.	James is more studious than intelligent.
Ci sono meno bambini in campagna che in città.	There are fewer children in the country than in the city.

If the second term of the comparison is expressed by a clause, *di quello che* must be used.

Studia può di quello che tu pensi.	He studies more than you think.

If the second term of the comparison is expressed by a pronoun, the object form is used:

Lui è più alto di me.	He is taller than I.
Io sono meno ricco di te.	I am less rich than you.
Lei è coraggiosa comme lui.	She is as brave as he.

SPECIAL USES OF THE COMPARATIVE

Some expressions with the comparative:

ancora del (dello, della, dei, etc.)	more
un po' più di	a little more
altro, -a, -i, -e	more
Voglio ancora del pane.	I want more bread.
Prendo un po' più di carne.	I take a little more meat.
Compriamo altri libri.	We buy more books.
non di più	no more (quantity)
non più	no longer (time)
Volete di più? No, non ne vogliamo di piu.	Do you want more? No, we don't want any more.
Lei non canta più.	She doesn't sing any more.
Tanto meglio!	Great! (So much the better.)
Tanto peggio!	Too bad! (So much the worse.)

11. RELATIVE SUPERLATIVE

The relative superlative (the most/the least/the . . . -est) is formed by placing the appropriate definite article before *più* or *meno*. Of/in is translated with *di*, whether by itself or combined with the definite article:

Quest' uomo è il più ricco del mondo.	This man is the richest in the world.
Lei è la più famosa delle sorelle.	She is the most famous of the sisters.
Marco è il meno timido di tutti.	Marco is the least timid of all.

The subjunctive often follows the superlative:

È il quadro più bello che io abbia mai visto.	It's the most beautiful painting I have ever seen.

With the superlative of adverbs, the definite article is often omitted, unless *possibile* is added to the adverb:

Parla più chiaramente di tutti.	She speaks the most clearly of all.
Parliamo il più chiaramente possibile.	We're speaking as clearly as possible.

12. ABSOLUTE SUPERLATIVE

1. The absolute superlative is formed by dropping the last vowel of the adjective and adding *-issimo, -issima, -issimi, -issime:*

L'esercizio è facilissimo.	The exercise is very easy.

2. By putting the words *molto, troppo,* or *assai* in front of the adjectives:

La poesia è molto bella.   The poem is very beautiful.

3. By using a second adjective of almost the same meaning, or by repeating the adjective:

La casa è piena zeppa di amici.   The house is full of (loaded with) friends.

La macchina è nuova nuova.   The car is brand new.

4. By using *stra-, arci-, sopra-, super-, extra-:*

Il signore è straricco. (or)   The gentleman is loaded with
Il signore è arciricco.   money.

Questa seta è sopraffina.   This silk is extra fine.

13. IRREGULAR COMPARATIVES AND SUPERLATIVES

Some adjectives and adverbs have irregular comparatives and superlatives in addition to the regular forms.

ADJECTIVE	COMPARATIVE	SUPERLATIVE
good	better	the best
buono(a)	*più buono(a)*	*il più buono*
	migliore	*buonissimo(a)*
		ottimo(a)
		il/la migliore
bad	worse	the worst
cattivo(a)	*peggiore*	*il/la peggiore*
	più cattivo(a)	*il/la più cattivo(a)*
		pessimo(a)
		cattivissimo(a)

big/great	bigger/greater	the biggest/greatest
grande	*maggiore*	*il/la maggiore*
	più grande	*grandissimo(a)*
		il/la più grande
		massimo(a)

small/little	smaller/lesser	the smallest
piccolo(a)	*minore*	*il/la minore*
	più piccolo(a)	*il/la più piccolo(a)*
		piccolissimo(a)
		minimo(a)

ADVERB	COMPARATIVE	SUPERLATIVE
well	better	the best
bene	*meglio*	*il meglio*
badly	worse	the worst
male	*peggio*	*il peggio*

14. DIMINUTIVES AND AUGMENTATIVES

1. The endings *-ino, -ina, -ello, -ella, -etto, -etta, -uccio, -uccia* imply smallness:

gattino	kitty
casetta	small house

2. The endings *-one, -ona, -otta* imply largeness:

stupidone	big fool
donnona	big woman

3. The endings *-ino, -uccio* indicate endearment:

tesoruccio	little treasure
boccuccia	sweet little mouth

4. The endings *-accio, -accia, -astro, -astra, -azzo, -azza*
   indicate depreciation:

parolaccia	curse word
cagnaccio	ugly dog

15. Masculine and Feminine

Nouns referring to males are masculine; nouns referring to females are feminine:

il padre	the father	*la madre*	the mother
il figlio	the son	*la figlia*	the daughter
l'uomo	the man	*la donna*	the woman
il toro	the bull	*la vacca*	the cow
il gatto	the tomcat	*la gatta*	the female cat

MASCULINE NOUNS

1. Nouns ending in *-o* are usually masculine:

il corpo	the body
il cielo	the sky
il denaro	the money

2. The names of the months and the names of the days (except Sunday) are masculine:

il gennaio scorso	last January
il lunedì	on Mondays

3. The names of lakes and some names of mountains are masculine:

il Garda	Lake Garda
gli Appennini	the Apennines

FEMININE NOUNS

Nouns ending in -*a* are usually feminine:

la testa	the head
la città	the city
la macchina	the car

NOUNS ENDING IN -*E*

Nouns ending in -*e* in the singular may be either masculine or feminine:

la madre	the mother
il padre	the father
la legge	the law
il piede	the foot

NOUNS WITH MASCULINE AND FEMININE FORMS

1. Some masculine nouns ending in -*a*, -*e*, -*o*, mostly professions, form their feminine in -*essa:*

il poeta	the poet	*la poetessa*	the poetess
il professore	the professor	*la professoressa*	the (female) professor

2. Masculine nouns ending in -*tore* form their feminine in -*trice:*

l'attore	the actor	*l'attrice*	the actress

16. PLURALS OF NOUNS

1. Nouns ending in *-o,* mostly masculine, form their plural in *-i:*

il bambino	the child	*i bambini*	the children

SOME EXCEPTIONS

A few nouns ending in *-o* are feminine:

la mano	the hand	*le mani*	the hands
la radio	the radio	*le radio*	the radios
la dinamo	the dynamo	*le dinamo*	the dynamos

Some masculine nouns ending in *-o* have two plurals, with different meanings for each plural:

il braccio	the arm
i bracci	the arms (of a stream)
le braccia	the arms (of the body)

2. Nouns ending in *-a,* usually feminine, form their plural in *-e:*

la rosa	the rose	*le rose*	the roses

Masculine nouns ending in *-a* form their plural in *-i:*

il poeta	the poet	*i poeti*	the poets

3. Nouns ending in *-e,* which can be masculine or feminine, form their plural in *-i:*

il nipote	the nephew or grandson	*i nipoti*	the nephews or grandsons

| *la nipote* | the niece or granddaughter | *le nipoti* | the nieces or granddaughters |

SPECIAL CASES

1. Nouns ending in *-ca* or *-ga* insert *h* in the plural in order to keep the "k" and "g" sound in the plural:

| *la barca* | the boat | *le barche* | the boats |
| *il monarca* | the monarch | *i monarchi* | the monarchs |

Exceptions:

| *un belga* | a Belgian | *i belgi* | the Belgians |
| *un amico* | a friend | *gli amici* | the friends |

2. Nouns ending in *-cia* or *-gia* (with unaccented *i*) form their plural in *-ce* or *-ge* if the *c* or *g* is double or is preceded by another consonant:

| *la spiaggia* | the seashore | *le spiagge* | the seashores |
| *la guancia* | the cheek | *le guance* | the cheeks |

Nouns ending in *-cia* or *-gia* form their plural in *-cie* or *-gie* if *c* or *g* is preceded by a vowel or if the *i* is accented:

| *la bugia* | the lie | *le bugie* | the lies |

3. Nouns ending in *-io* (without an accent on the *i*) have a single *i* in the plural:

| *il figlio* | the son | *i figli* | the sons |

If the *i* is accented, the plural has *ii:*

| *lo zio* | the uncle | *gli zii* | the uncles |

4. Nouns ending in *-co* or *-go* form their plural in *-chi* or *-ghi* if the accent falls on the syllable before the last:

il fico	the fig	*i fichi*	the figs

Exception:

l' amico	the friend	*gli amici*	the friends

If the accent falls on the second-to-last syllable, the plural is in *-ci* or *-gi:*

il medico	the doctor	*i medici*	the doctors

5. Nouns in the singular with the accent on the last vowel do not change in the plural:

la città	the city	*le città*	the cities

17. DAYS OF THE WEEK

The days of the week (except Sunday) are masculine and are not capitalized unless they begin a sentence. The article is only used when referring to a repeated, habitual event, as in "on Sundays" "on Mondays," etc.

lunedì	Monday
martedì	Tuesday
mercoledì	Wednesday
giovedì	Thursday
venerdì	Friday
sabato	Saturday
domenica	Sunday
Vengo lunedì.	I'm coming on Monday.
Gli andranno a fare visita domenica.	They're going to pay them a visit on Sunday.

La vedo sabato.	I'll see her on Saturday.
La domenica vado in chiesa.	On Sundays I go to church.
Vado a scuola il venerdì.	I go to school on Fridays.

Note: The word *on* is not translated before the days of the week or a date.

il 15 febbraio	on February 15

18. MONTHS OF THE YEAR

The names of the months are masculine and are not capitalized unless they begin a sentence. They are usually used without the definite article:

gennaio	January
febbraio	February
marzo	March
aprile	April
maggio	May
giugno	June
luglio	July
agosto	August
settembre	September
ottobre	October
novembre	November
dicembre	December

19. THE SEASONS

l'inverno (masc.)	winter
la primavera	spring
l'estate (fem.)	summer
l'autunno (masc.)	fall

The names of the seasons are usually not capitalized. They are preceded by the definite article, but after *di* the article may or may not be used:

L'inverno è una brutta stagione.	Winter is an ugly season.
Fa freddo d'inverno.	It's cold in (the) winter.
Io lavoro durante i mesi d'estate (or dell'estate).	I work during the summer months.

20. NUMBERS

The plural of *mille* (thousand) is *mila; duemila,* two thousand; *seimila,* six thousand.

After *milione* the preposition *di* is used:

un milione di soldati	one million soldiers
tre milioni di dollari	three million dollars

In writing a date, give the day first and then the month:

il 5 (cinque) agosto	August 5th
il 10 (dieci) novembre	November 10th

The ordinal numeral is used only for the first of the month:

il primo novembre	November 1st
il tre agosto	August 3rd

21. DEMONSTRATIVES

questo, -a, -i, -e	this, these
quello, -a, -i, -e	that, those

The pronoun "this" is *questo:*

Questo è l'uomo che cerchiamo.	This is the man we are looking for.

Besides the forms of *quello* already given, there are also the forms *quel, quei, quegli*. Here is how they are used:

1. If the article *il* is used before the noun, use *quel*:

il libro	the book
quel libro	that book

2. If the word begins with a vowel and the article *l'* is used, then use *quell'*:

l'orologio	the watch
quell'orologio	that watch

3. If *i* is used before the noun, use *quei*:

i maestri	the teachers
quei maestri	those teachers

4. If *gli* is used before the noun, use *quegli*:

gli studenti	the students
quegli studenti	those students

The same rules apply to *bel, bell', bei, begli*, from *bello, -a, -i, -e*, "beautiful."

22. POSSESSIVE ADJECTIVES

Always use the article in front of a possessive adjective:

il mio denaro	my money
la tua sedia	your chair
la vostra borsa	your pocketbook

Except for members of the family in the singular:

mia madre	my mother

The possessive adjective agrees with the thing possessed and not with the possessor:

la sua casa   (his, her) house

Suo may mean *his* or *her*, or, with the polite form, *your*. If confusion should arise because of the use of *suo*, use *di lui*, *di lei*, etc.

23. INDEFINITE ADJECTIVES

1. *qualche* (used only in *sing.*)	some
alcuni (used only in *pl.*)	some

qualche lettera   some letters
alcuni dollari   some dollars

2. *qualunque, qualsiasi* (has no *pl.*)	any

qualunque mese   any month
qualsiasi ragazzo   any boy

3. *ogni* (has no *pl.*)	every or each
ciascun, ciascuno, ciascuna (no *pl.*)	each or every

Ogni ragazzo parla.   Every boy talks.
Ogni ragazza parla.   Every girl talks.
Diciamo una parola a   Let's say a word to each
   ciascun signore.   gentlemen.
Raccontate tutto a   Tell everything to each
   ciascuna signora.   (or every) woman.

4. *altro (l'altro), altra, altri, altre* — other or more

Mandiamo gli altri libri? — Do we send the other books?

Vuole altro denaro? — Do you want more money?

5. *nessuno, nessun, nessuna* — no, no one

Nessuno zio ha scritto. — No uncle wrote.
Nessun soldato ha paura. — No soldier is afraid.
Nessuna sedia è buona. — No chair is good.

24. INDEFINITE PRONOUNS

1. *alcuni* — some
   alcuni . . . altri — some . . . some

alcuni dei suoi discorsi — some of his speeches
Di questi libri, alcuni sono buoni, altri cattivi. — Of these books, some are good, some bad.

2. *qualcuno* — someone, somebody

Qualcuno è venuto. — Somebody came.

3. *chiunque* (no *fem.*, no *pl.*) — anybody, any one

Chiunque dice così. — Anybody says so.

4. *ognuno* (only *sing.*); *tutti* (only *pl.*) — each one, each person; everybody, everyone
   ciascuno (only *sing.*); *tutto* — each or each one; everything

Tutti corrono.	Everybody runs. (All run.)
Ho dato un biscotto ciascuno.	I gave each a cookie.

5. *l' altro, l' altra, gli altri, le altre, altro*

the other, the others; (in interrogative or negative sentences) else, anything else

   un altro

another one

Lui dice una cosa ma l' altro non è d' accordo.	He says one thing, but the other one does not agree.
Volete altro?	Do you want something else?
Non vogliamo altro.	We do not want anything else.

6. *niente, nulla*

nothing

   nessuno (no *fem.*, no *pl.*)

nobody, no one

Niente (nulla) lo consola.	Nothing consoles him.
Nessuno conosce questa regola.	Nobody knows this rule.

25. Interrogative Pronouns and Adjectives

1. The interrogative pronoun *chi* refers to persons, and corresponds to *who, whom,* or *which,* as illustrated by the three examples following:

Chi vi scrive?	Who writes to you?
Chi vediamo?	Whom do we see?
Chi di noi ha parlato?	Which one of us has talked?

2. *Che, cosa,* or *che cosa* translates as *what:*

Che facciamo?	What are we going to do?
Che cosa leggete?	What are you reading?
Cosa studi?	What do you study [in college]?

3. The two interrogative adjectives *quale* and *che* mean *which, what:*

Quale dei due giornali compra Lei?	Which of the two newspapers do you buy?
Che colore desiderate?	What color do you want?

26. RELATIVE PRONOUNS

chi	he who, him who
che	who, whom, that, which
cui	(used with prepositions)
a cui	to whom
di cui	of whom, of which
in cui	in which

Chi studia impara.	He who studies, learns.
l'uomo che ho visto	the man whom I saw
la donna di cui parlo	the woman of whom I speak
la ragazza a cui parlo	the girl to whom I'm speaking

1. *che* (undeclinable): For masculine, feminine, singular, plural; for persons, animals, things. Do not use this pronoun if there is a preposition.

2. *il quale, la quale, i quali, le quali:* For persons, animals, things, with the same English meanings as *che;*

can be used with or without prepositions. When used with prepositions, the contracted forms are used, e.g., *alla quale, dei quali,* etc.

3. *cui* (undeclinable): Masculine, feminine, singular, plural; for persons, animals, things; substitutes *che* when there is a preposition (*di, a, da, in, con, su, per, fra*)

27. PERSONAL PRONOUNS

Pronouns have different forms depending on whether they are:

1. The subject of a verb
2. The direct object of a verb
3. The indirect object of a verb
4. Used after a preposition
5. Used with reflexive verbs

a. The subject pronouns are:

SINGULAR

io	I
tu	you *(fam.)*
lui	he
lei	she
Lei	you *(pol.)*
esso	it *(masc.)*
essa	it *(fem.)*

PLURAL

noi	we
voi	you
loro	they
Loro	you *(formal plur.)*

It is not necessary to use subject pronouns as the verb ending indicates who is speaking or being spoken about.

b. The direct object pronouns are:

mi	me
ti	you *(fam.)*
lo	him, it
la	her, it, you *(pol.)*
ci	us
vi	you
li	them, you
le	them, you

Ci vede.	He sees us.
Lo scrive.	He writes it.

c. The indirect object pronouns are:

mi	to me
ti	to you *(fam.)*
gli	to him
le	to her
Le	to you *(pol.)*
ci	to us
vi	to you
gli/aloro	to them, to you *(form.)*

Lui mi scrive una lettera.	He is writing me a letter.
Io ti regalo una bambola.	I am giving you a doll.
Noi gli parliamo.	We speak to them.

d. The pronouns used after a preposition are:

me	me
te	you *(fam.)*

lui	him
lei	her, you *(pol.)*
noi	us
voi	you
loro	them, you *(form.)*

Io verrò con te.	I will come with you.
Lui parla sempre di lei.	He always speaks about her.

e. The reflexive pronouns are:

mi	myself
ti	yourself *(fam.)*
si	himself, herself, itself, yourself *(pol.)*
ci	ourselves
vi	yourselves
si	themselves, yourselves *(form.)*

Io mi lavo.	I wash myself.
Noi ci alziamo alle nove.	We get up at nine.
Loro si alzano.	They get up.

28. POSITION OF PRONOUNS

1. Pronouns are written as separate words, before the verb, except with the imperative, infinitive, and gerund, where they follow the verbal form and are written as one word with it:

Ditelo.	Say it.
Fatemi un favore.	Do me a favor.
facendolo . . .	doing it . . .
chiamandolo	calling him
per scriverle una lettera	to write her a letter
dopo avermi chiamato	after having called me

2. In the imperative, when the polite form is used, the pronouns are never attached to the verb:

Mi faccia un favore.   Do me a favor.

3. Some verbs of one syllable in the imperative double the initial consonant of the pronoun:

Dimmi una cosa.   Tell me one thing.
Facci una cortesia.   Do us a favor.

4. In the compound infinitive the pronoun is generally attached to the auxiliary:

Credo di averti dato tutto.   I think I gave you everything.

The simple infinitive drops the final *e* before the pronoun:

per leggere un articolo   to read an article
per leggerti un articolo   to read you an article

5. When two object pronouns are used with the same verb, the indirect precedes the direct:

Te lo voglio dire.   I want to tell it to you.

Observe the following changes in the pronouns that occur in this case:

The *i* in *mi, ti, ci, vi, si* changes to *e* before *lo, la, le, li, ne,* while *gli* takes an additional *e* and is written as one word with the following pronoun. *Le* also becomes *glie* before *lo, la, li, le, ne:*

Ce lo dà.   He gives it to us.
Glielo mando a casa.   I send it to him (to her,
                                 to you) at home.
Glielo dicono.   They tell it to him (to her, to
                                 you, to them).

29. NE

1. Used as a pronoun meaning *of him, of her, of them, of it:*

Parla del mio amico?	Are you talking of my friend?
Sì ne parlo.	Yes, I am talking of him.
Parliamo di questa cosa?	Are we talking of this thing?
Sì, ne parliamo.	Yes, we are talking of it.

2. Used as a partitive meaning "some" or "any":

Mangia del pesce la signorina?	Does the young lady eat some fish?
Sì, ne mangia.	Yes, she does (eat some).

30. SI

1. *Si* can be used as a reflexive pronoun:

Lui si lava.	He washes himself.
Loro si lavano.	They wash themselves.

2. *Si* is used as an impersonal pronoun:

Non sempre si riflette su quel che si dice.	Not always does one ponder over what one says.
Qui si mangia bene.	Here one eats well.

3. *Si* is sometimes used to translate the English passive:

Come si manda questa lettera?	How is this letter sent?

31. ADVERBS

1. Many adverbs end in *-mente:*

caramente	dearly
dolcemente	sweetly

These adverbs are easily formed; take the feminine, singular form of the adjective and add *-mente*. For instance, "dear" = *caro, cara, cari, care;* the feminine singular is *cara*, and so the adverb will be *caramente*. "Sweet" is *dolce, dolci* (there is no difference between the masculine and feminine); the feminine singular is *dolce*, and so the adverb will be *dolcemente*.

2. Adjectives ending in *-le* or *-re* drop the final *e* before *-mente* if the *l* or *r* is preceded by a vowel; thus the adverb corresponding to *facile* is *facilmente* (easily). The adverbs corresponding to *buono* (good) and *cattivo* (bad) are *bene* and *male*.

3. Adverbs may have a comparative and superlative form: *Caramente, più caramente, molto caramente,* or *carissimamente*.

Observe these irregular comparative and superlative forms of adverbs:

meglio	better
peggio	worse
maggiormente	more greatly
massimamente	very greatly
minimamente	in the least
ottimamente	very well
pessimamente	very bad

32. PREPOSITIONS

1. The most common prepositions in Italian are:

di	of
a	at, to
da	from

in	in
con	with
su	above
per	through, by means of, on
tra, fra	between, among

2. When used before a definite article, these prepositions are often contracted. Here are the most common of these combinations:

di + il = del	*a + il = al*
di + lo = dello	*a + lo = allo*
di + la = della	*a + la = alla*
di + l' = dell'	*a + l' = all'*
di + i = dei	*a + i = ai*
di + gli = degli	*a + gli = agli*
di + le = delle	*a + le = alle*
con + il = col	*sul + il = sul*
con + i = coi	*su + la = sulla*
	su + lo = sullo
	su + gli = sugli
	su + i = sui

Io ho del denaro.	I have some money.
il cavallo dello zio	the uncle's horse
Io regalo un dollaro al ragazzo.	I give a dollar to the boy.
Il professore risponde agli studenti.	The professor answers the students.

33. NEGATION

1. *Non* (not) comes before the verb:

Io non vedo.	I don't see.
Lui non parla.	He isn't speaking.

2. Nothing, never, no one:

Non vedo nulla.	I see nothing.
Non vado mai.	I never go.
Non viene nessuno.	No one comes.

If the negative pronoun begins the sentence, *non* is not used.

Nessuno viene.	No one comes.

34. Question Words

Che?	What?
Che cosa?	What?
Perchè?	Why?
Come?	How?
Quanto?	How much?
Quando?	When?
Dove?	Where?
Quale?	Which?

35. The Tenses of Verbs

Italian verbs are divided into three classes (conjugations) according to their infinitives:

Class I—*parlare, amare*
Class II—*scrivere, temere*
Class III—*partire, sentire*

1. The present:
   To form the present tense, take off the infinitive ending (*-are, -ere, -ire*) and add the following present tense endings:

First Conj. (I)	Second Conj. (II)	Third Conj. (III)
-o	*-o*	*-o*
-i	*-i*	*-i*

-a	*-e*	*-e*
-iamo	*-iamo*	*-iamo*
-ate	*-ete*	*-ite*
-ano	*-ono*	*-ono*

The present tense can be translated in several ways:

Io parlo italiano.	I speak Italian. I am speaking Italian. I do speak Italian.

2. The imperfect:

I	II	III
-avo	*-evo*	*-ivo*
-avi	*-evi*	*-ivi*
-ava	*-eva*	*-iva*
-avamo	*-evamo*	*-ivamo*
-avate	*-evate*	*-ivate*
-avano	*-evano*	*-ivano*

The imperfect is used:

a. To indicate continued or customary action in the past:

Quando ero a Roma andavo sempre a visitare i musei.	When I was in Rome, I was always visiting the museums.
Lo incontravo ogni giorno.	I used to meet him every day./I would meet him every day.

b. To indicate what was happening when something else happened:

Lui scriveva quando lei è entrata.	He was writing when she entered.

3. The future:
   The future of regular verbs is formed by adding to the infinitive (after the final *e* is dropped) the endings -*ò;* -*ai;* -*à;* -*emo;* -*ete;* -*anno.* For the first conjugation, the *a* of the infinitive changes to *e.*

   The future generally expresses actions that will take place in the future:

Lo comprerò.	I'll buy it.
Andrò domani.	I'll go tomorrow.

   Sometimes it expresses probability or conjecture:

Che ora sarà?	What time can it be? What time do you think it must be?
Sarà l'una.	It must be one.
Starà mangiando ora.	He's probably eating now.

4. *Passato remoto* (preterit, past definite):
   This tense indicates an action that happened in a period of time completely finished now. Although there are some regions in Italy where the *passato remoto* is used in conversation, it is chiefly a literary tense, and the *passato prossimo* is used in conversation instead.

Romolo fondò Roma.	Romulus founded Rome.
Dante nacque nel 1265.	Dante was born in 1265.
Garibaldi combattè per l'unità d'Italia.	Garibaldi fought for the unity of Italy.

5. *Passato prossimo* (compound past):
   The *passato prossimo* is formed by adding the past participle to the present indicative of *avere* or *essere.* It is used to indicate a past action and corresponds to the English preterit or present perfect:

Io ho finito il mio lavoro.	I finished my work. (I have finished my work.)

| *L'hai visto?* | Have you seen him? |
| *Sono arrivati.* | They arrived. |

6. The past perfect tense is formed by adding the past participle to the imperfect of *avere* or *essere*.

| *Lui l'aveva fatto.* | He had done it. |

7. The *trapassato remoto* (preterit perfect) is formed by adding the past participle to the past definite of *avere* or *essere*. It is a rare, literary tense used to indicate an event that had happened just before another event:

| *Quando uscì ebbe finito.* | When he went out, he had finished. |

8. The future perfect tense is a literary tense formed by adding the past participle to the future of *avere* or *essere*.

| *Lui avrà finito presto.* | He will soon have finished. |

The future perfect can also be used to indicate probability:

| *Lui sarà stato ammalato.* | He was probably sick. |
| *Saranno già partiti.* | They probably left already. |

Complete conjugation of a sample verb from each class:

AMARE (FIRST CONJUGATION): TO LOVE, TO LIKE

INDICATIVE

PRESENT	IMPERFECT
io amo	*io amavo*
tu ami	*tu amavi*
lui/lei/Lei ama	*lui/lei/Lei amava*

noi amiamo
voi amate
loro amano

noi amavamo
voi amavate
loro amavano

FUTURE

io amerò
tu amerai
lui/lei/Lei amerà
noi ameremo
voi amerete
loro ameranno

PRESENT PERFECT

io ho amato
tu hai amato
lui/lei/Lei ha amato
noi abbiamo amato
voi avete amato
loro hanno amato

PRETERIT

io amai
tu amasti
lui/lei/Lei amò
noi amammo
voi amaste
loro amarono

PAST PERFECT

io avevo amato
tu avevi amato
lui/lei/Lei aveva amato
noi avevamo amato
voi avevate amato
loro avevano amato

PRETERIT PERFECT

io ebbi amato
tu avesti amato
lui/lei/Lei ebbe amato
noi avemmo amato
voi aveste amato
loro ebbero amato

FUTURE PERFECT

io avrò amato
tu avrai amato
lui/lei/Lei avrà amato
noi avremo amato
voi avrete amato
loro avranno amato

SUBJUNCTIVE

PRESENT

che io ami
che tu ami
che lui/lei/Lei ami
che noi amiamo
che voi amiate
che loro amino

IMPERFECT

che io amassi
che tu amassi
che lui/lei/Lei amasse
che noi amassimo
che voi amaste
che loro amassero

PERFECT	PAST PERFECT
che io abbia amato	*che io avessi amato*
che tu abbia amato	*che tu avessi amato*
che lui/lei/Lei abbia amato	*che lui/lei/Lei avesse amato*
che noi abbiamo amato	*che noi avessimo amato*
che voi abbiate amato	*che voi aveste amato*
che lui abbiano amato	*che loro avessero amato*

IMPERATIVE

PRESENT
ama (tu)
ami (Lei)
amiamo (noi)
amate (voi)
amino (Loro)

CONDITIONAL

PRESENT	PERFECT
io amerei	*io avrei amato*
tu ameresti	*tu avresti amato*
lui/lei/Lei amerebbe	*lui/lei/Lei avrebbe amato*
noi ameremmo	*noi avremmo amato*
voi amereste	*voi avreste amato*
loro amerebbero	*loro avrebbero amato*

INFINITIVES

PRESENT	PERFECT
amare	*avere amato*

PARTICIPLES

PRESENT	PERFECT
amante	*amato*

GERUNDS

PRESENT	PERFECT
amando	*avendo amato*

TEMERE (SECOND CONJUGATION): TO FEAR

INDICATIVE

PRESENT
io temo
tu temi
lui/lei/Lei teme
noi temiamo
voi temete
loro temono

IMPERFECT
io temevo
tu temevi
lui/lei/Lei temeva
noi temevamo
voi temevate
loro temevano

FUTURE
io temerò
tu temerai
lui/lei/Lei temerà
noi temeremo
voi temerete
loro temeranno

PRESENT PERFECT
io ho temuto
tu hai temuto
lui/lei/Lei ha temuto
noi abbiamo temuto
voi avete temuto
loro hanno temuto

PRETERIT
io temei (or -etti)
tu temesti
lui/lei/Lei temè (or -ette)
noi tememmo
voi temeste
loro temerono (or -ettero)

PAST PERFECT
io avevo temuto
tu avevi temuto
lui/lei/Lei aveva temuto
noi avevamo temuto
voi avevate temuto
loro avevano temuto

PRETERIT PERFECT
io ebbi temuto
tu avesti temuto
lui/lei/Lei ebbe temuto
noi avemmo temuto
voi aveste temuto
loro ebbero temuto

FUTURE PERFECT
io avrò temuto
tu avrai temuto
lui/lei/Lei avrà temuto
noi avremo temuto
voi avrete temuto
loro avranno temuto

SUBJUNCTIVE

PRESENT	IMPERFECT
che io tema	*che io temessi*
che tu tema	*che tu temessi*
che lui/lei/Lei tema	*che lui/lei/Lei temesse*
che noi temiamo	*che noi temessimo*
che voi temiate	*che voi temeste*
che loro temano	*che loro temessero*

PERFECT	PAST PERFECT
che io abbia temuto	*che io avessi temuto*
che tu abbia temuto	*che tu avessi temuto*
che lui/lei/Lei abbia temuto	*che lui/lei/Lei avesse temuto*
che noi abbiamo temuto	*che noi avessimo temuto*
che voi abbiate temuto	*che voi aveste temuto*
che loro abbiano temuto	*che loro avessero temuto*

IMPERATIVE

PRESENT
temi (tu)
tema (Lei)
temiamo (noi)
temete (voi)
temano (Loro)

CONDITIONAL

PRESENT	PERFECT
io temerei	*io avrei temuto*
tu temeresti	*tu avresti temuto*
lui/lei/Lei temerebbe	*lui/lei/Lei avrebbe temuto*
noi temeremmo	*noi avremmo temuto*
voi temereste	*voi avreste temuto*
loro temerebbero	*loro avrebbero temuto*

INFINITIVES

PRESENT
temere

PERFECT
aver temuto

PARTICIPLES

PRESENT
temente

PERFECT
temuto

GERUNDS

PRESENT
temendo

PERFECT
avendo temuto

Sentire (Third Conjugation): to hear

INDICATIVE

PRESENT
io sento
tu senti
lui/lei/Lei sente
noi sentiamo
voi sentite
loro sentono

IMPERFECT
io sentivo
tu sentivi
lui/lei/Lei sentiva
noi sentivamo
voi sentivate
loro sentivano

FUTURE
io sentirò
tu sentirai
lui/lei/Lei sentirà
noi sentiremo
voi sentirete
loro sentiranno

PRESENT PERFECT
io ho sentito
tu hai sentito
lui/lei/Lei ha sentito
noi abbiamo sentito
voi avete sentito
loro hanno sentito

PRETERIT	PAST PERFECT
io sentii	*io avevo sentito*
tu sentisti	*tu avevi sentito*
lui/lei/Lei sentì	*lui/lei/Lei aveva sentito*
noi sentimmo	*noi avevamo sentito*
voi sentiste	*voi avevate sentito*
loro sentirono	*loro avevano sentito*

PRETERIT PERFECT	FUTURE PERFECT
io ebbi sentito	*io avrò sentito*
tu avesti sentito	*tu avrai sentito*
lui/lei/Lei ebbe sentito	*lui/lei/Lei avrà sentito*
noi avemmo sentito	*noi avremo sentito*
voi aveste sentito	*voi avrete sentito*
loro ebbero sentito	*loro avranno sentito*

SUBJUNCTIVE

PRESENT	IMPERFECT
che io senta	*che io sentissi*
che tu senta	*che tu sentissi*
che lui/lei/Lei senta	*che lui/lei/Lei sentisse*
che noi sentiamo	*che noi sentissimo*
che voi sentiate	*che voi sentiste*
che loro sentano	*che loro sentissero*

PERFECT	PAST PERFECT
che io abbia sentito	*che io avessi sentito*
che tu abbia sentito	*che tu avessi sentito*
che lui/lei/Lei abbia sentito	*che lui/lei/Lei avesse sentito*
che noi abbiamo sentito	*che noi avessimo sentito*
che voi abbiate sentito	*che voi aveste sentito*
che loro abbiano sentito	*che loro avessero sentito*

IMPERATIVE

PRESENT
senti (tu)
senta (Lei)
sentiamo (noi)
sentite (voi)
sentano (Loro)

CONDITIONAL

PRESENT
io sentirei
tu sentiresti
lui/lei/Lei sentirebbe
noi sentiremmo
voi sentireste
loro sentirebbero

PERFECT
io avrei sentito
tu avresti sentito
lui/lei/Lei avrebbe sentito
noi avremmo sentito
voi avreste sentito
loro avrebbero sentito

INFINITIVES

PRESENT
sentire

PERFECT
aver sentito

PARTICIPLES

PRESENT
sentente

PERFECT
sentito

GERUNDS

PRESENT
sentendo

PERFECT
avendo sentito

36. The Past Participle

1. The past participle ends in:

-ato, (-ata, -ati, -ate)   *parl -ato*
  (for the First Conjugation)

-uto (-uta, -uti, -ute)   *bev -uto*
  (for the Second Conjugation)

-ito (-ita, -iti, -ite)   *part -ito*
  (for the Third Conjugation)

2. The past participle used with *essere* agrees with the
   subject of the verb:

Marco è andato.	Marco left.
Le bambine sono andate.	The girls left.

All reflexive verbs also conjugate with *essere*.

Mi sono divertito/a.	I enjoyed myself (f./m.).

3. The past participle used with *avere* changes its form
   only when it follows a direct object pronoun with
   which it must agree.

Ho comprato i CD.	I bought the CDs.
Li ho comprati.	I bought them.
Ho visto Anna.	I saw Anna.
L'ho vista.	I saw her.

37. USE OF THE AUXILIARIES

The most common intransitive verbs that are conjugated with the verb *essere* in the compound tenses are the following:

andare, arrivare, scendere, entrare, salire, morire, nascere, partire, restare, ritornare, uscire, cadere, venire.

Io sono venuto (-a).	I have come.
Lui è arrivato.	He has arrived.
Noi siamo partiti.	We have left.

Reflexive verbs form their compound tenses with *essere*. The past participle agrees with the subject.

La signorina si è rotta il braccio.	The young lady broke her arm.

The past tenses of passive constructions are formed with *essere:*

Il ragazzo è amato.	The boy is loved.
La ragazza è stata amata.	The girl has been loved.
I ragazzi furono amati.	The boys were loved.
Le ragazze saranno amate.	The girls will be loved.

Sometimes the verb *venire* is used instead of *essere* in a passive construction:

La poesia è letta dal maestro.	The poem is read by the teacher.
La poesia viene letta dal maestro.	The poem is read by the teacher.

38. THE PRESENT PROGRESSIVE

Io fumo means "I smoke" or "I am smoking," but there is also a special way of translating "I am smoking": *Io sto fumando*. In other words, Italian uses the verb *stare* with the present gerund of the main verb to emphasize that an action is in progress:

Noi stiamo leggendo.	We are reading.
Lui stava scrivendo.	He was writing.

This form is generally used only in the simple tenses.

39. THE SUBJUNCTIVE

Formation

1. The present tense

   a. First Conjugation: by dropping the *-are* from the infinitive and adding *-i, -i, -i, -iamo, -iate, -ino*.

Penso che lui parli troppo.	I think (that) he speaks too much.

   b. Second and Third Conjugations: by dropping the *-ere* and *-ire* and adding *-a, -a, -a, -iamo, -iate, -iano*.

Sebbene Lei scriva in fretta non fa errori.	Although you write fast, you make no mistakes.

2. The imperfect tense

   a. First Conjugation: by dropping the *-are* and adding *-assi, -assi, -asse, -assimo, -aste, -assero*.

Credevo che il ragazzo lavorasse molto.	I thought (that) the boy was working hard.

b. Second Conjugation: by dropping the *-ere* and adding *-essi, -essi, -esse, -essimo, -este, -essero*.

Prima che le signorina scrivesse la lettera il padre la chiamò.	Before the girl wrote the letter, her father called her.

c. Third Conjugation: by dropping the *-ire* and adding *-issi, -issi, -isse, -issimo, -iste, -issero*.

Ero del parere che il mio amico si sentisse male.	I was under the impression that my friend did not feel well.

3. The compound tenses (perfect and past perfect)
   These are formed with the present and imperfect of the subjunctive of "to have" and "to be" and the past participle.

Credo che gli studenti abbiano finito la lezione.	I think (that) the students have finished the lesson.
Era possibile che i mei amici fossero già arrivati in città.	It was possible that my friends had already arrived in town.

Uses of the Subjunctive

The subjunctive mood expresses doubt, uncertainty, hope, fear, desire, supposition, possibility, probability, granting, etc. For this reason, it is mostly found in clauses dependent upon another verb.

The subjunctive is used in dependent clauses in the following ways:

a. After verbs expressing hope, wish, desire, command, doubt:

Voglio che tu ci vada.	I want you to go there.

    b. After verbs expressing an opinion *(penso, credo):*

Penso che sia vero.	I think it is true.

    c. After expressions made with a form of *essere* and an adjective or an adverb *(è necessario, è facile, è possibile),* or some impersonal expressions like *bisogna, importa, etc.:*

È necessario che io parta subito.	It is necessary that I leave immediately.
È impossibile che noi veniamo questa sera.	It is impossible for us to come this evening.

    d. After some conjunctions—*sebbene, quantunque, per quanto, benchè, affinchè, prima che* (subjunctive to express a possibility; indicative to express a fact):

Sebbene non sia guarito, devo uscire.	Although I am not well yet, I must go out.
Benche io te l' abbia già detto, ricordati di andare alla Posta.	Although I told you already, remember to go to the Post Office.

40. THE CONDITIONAL

The conditional is formed:

1. In the present tense:

    a. First and Second Conjugations: by dropping the *-are,* or *-ere* and adding *-erei, -ereste, -erebbe, -eremmo, -ereste, -erebbero.*

La signora parlerebbe molto, se potesse.	The lady would speak a lot if she could.

    b. Third Conjugation: by dropping the *-ire* and adding
       -irei, -iresti, -irebbe, -iremmo, -ireste, -irebbero.

Il signore si sentirebbe bene,	The gentleman would feel
se prendesse le pillole.	well if he took the pills.

2. In the past tense:
    By using the present conditional of "to have" or "to
    be" and the past participle.

Mio cugino non avrebbe	My cousin would not have
investito il suo denaro in	invested his money in this
questo, se l' avesse saputo	if he had known it before.
prima.	

41. "IF" CLAUSES

An "if" clause can express:

1. *Reality.* In this case the indicative present and future is
    used:

Se studio, imparo.	If I study, I learn.
Se oggi pioverà, non	If it rains today, I won't
uscirò.	go out.

2. *Possibility.* The imperfect subjunctive and the condi-
    tional present are used to express possibility in the
    present:

Se studiassi, imparerei.	If I studied, I would learn.
Se tu leggessi, impareresti.	If you read, you would learn. (The idea is that it is possible that you may read and so you may learn.)

The past perfect subjunctive and the past conditional are used to express a possibility in the past:

Se tu avessi letto, avresti imparato.	If you had read, you would have learned. (The idea is that you might have read and so might have learned.)

3. *Impossibility* or *counterfactuality*. Use the same construction as in number 2; the only difference is that we know that the condition cannot be fulfilled.

Se avessi studiato, avrei imparato.	If I had studied, I would have learned. (But it's a fact that I did not study, and so I did not learn.)
Se l'uomo vivesse mille anni, imparerebbe molte cose.	If a man lived 1,000 years, he would learn many things. (But it's a fact that people don't live 1,000 years, and so don't learn many things.)

42. THE IMPERATIVE

The forms of the imperative are normally taken from the present indicative:

leggi	read (*familiar*)
leggiamo	let's read
leggete	read (*plural*)

For the First Conjugation, however, note:

canta	sing

The polite forms of the imperative are taken from the present subjunctive:

canti	sing
cantino	sing
legga	read
leggano	read

43. "To Be" and "To Have"

Essere and *avere*, "to be" and "to have," are very irregular. For your convenience, here are their complete conjugations.

ESSERE: TO BE

INDICATIVE

PRESENT	PRETERIT
io sono	*io fui*
tu sei	*tu fosti*
lui/lei/Lei è	*lui/lei/Lei fu*
noi siamo	*noi fummo*
voi siete	*voi foste*
loro sono	*loro furono*

IMPERFECT	PAST PERFECT
io ero	*io ero stato/a*
tu eri	*tu eri stato/a*
lui/lei/Lei era	*lui/lei/Lei era stato/a*
noi eravamo	*noi eravamo stati/e*
voi eravate	*voi eravate stati/e*
loro erano	*loro erano stati/e*

FUTURE	PRETERIT PERFECT
io sarò	*io fui stato/a*
tu sarai	*tu fosti stato/a*

lui/lei/Lei sarà	*lui/lei/Lei fu stato/a*
noi saremo	*noi fummo stati/e*
voi sarete	*voi foste stati/e*
loro saranno	*loro furono stati/e*

PRESENT PERFECT	FUTURE PERFECT
io sono stato/a	*io sarò stato/a*
tu sei stato/a	*tu sarai stato/a*
lui/lei/Lei è stato	*lui/lei/Lei sarà stato*
noi siamo stati/e	*noi saremo stati/e*
voi siete stati/e	*voi sarete stati/e*
loro sono stati/e	*loro saranno stati/e*

SUBJUNCTIVE

PRESENT	IMPERFECT
che io sia	*che io fossi*
che tu sia	*che tu fossi*
che lui/lei/Lei sia	*che lui/lei/Lei fosse*
che noi siamo	*che noi fossimo*
che voi siate	*che voi foste*
che loro siano	*che loro fossero*

PERFECT	PAST PERFECT
che io sia stato/a	*che io fossi stato/a*
che tu sia stato/a	*che tu fossi stato/a*
che lui/lei/Lei sia stato	*che lui/lei/Lei fosse stato/a*
che noi siamo stati/e	*che noi fossimo stati/e*
che voi siate stati/e	*che voi foste stati/e*
che loro siano stati/e	*che loro fossero stati/e*

IMPERATIVE

PRESENT
sii (tu)
sia (Lei)
siamo (noi)
siate (voi)
siano (Loro)

CONDITIONAL

PRESENT
io sarei
tu saresti
lui/lei/Lei sarebbe
noi saremmo
voi sareste
loro sarebbero

PERFECT
io sarei stato/a
tu saresti stato/a
lui/lei/Lei sarebbe stato/a
noi saremmo stati/e
voi sareste stati/e
loro sarebbero stati/e

INFINITIVE

PRESENT
essere

PERFECT
essere stato/a/i/e

PARTICIPLE

PERFECT
stato/a/i/e

GERUND

PRESENT
essendo

PERFECT
essendo stato/a/i/e

AVERE: TO HAVE

INDICATIVE

PRESENT
io ho
tu hai
lui/lei/Lei ha
noi abbiamo
voi avete
loro hanno

PRETERIT
io ebbi
tu avesti
lui/lei/Lei ebbe
noi avemmo
voi aveste
loro ebbero

IMPERFECT
io avevo
tu avevi

PAST PERFECT
io avevo avuto
tu avevi avuto

lui/lei/Lei aveva
noi avevamo
voi avevate
loro avevano

lui/lei/Lei aveva avuto
noi avevamo avuto
voi avevate avuto
loro avevano avuto

FUTURE
io avrò
tu avrai
lui/lei/Lei avrà
noi avremo
voi avrete
loro avranno

PRETERIT PERFECT
io ebbi avuto
tu avesti avuto
lui/lei/Lei ebbi avuto
noi avemmo avuto
voi aveste avuto
loro ebbero avuto

PRESENT PERFECT
io ho avuto
tu hai avuto
lui/lei/Lei ha avuto
noi abbiamo avuto
voi avete avuto
loro hanno avuto

FUTURE PERFECT
io avrò avuto
tu avrai avuto
lui/lei/Lei avrà avuto
noi avremo avuto
voi avrete avuto
loro avranno avuto

SUBJUNCTIVE

PRESENT
che io abbia
che tu abbia
che lui/lei/Lei abbia
che noi abbiamo
che voi abbiate
che loro abbiano

IMPERFECT
che io avessi
che tu avessi
che lui/lei/Lei avesse
che noi avessimo
che voi aveste
che loro avessero

PERFECT
che io abbia avuto
che tu abbia avuto
che lui/lei/Lei abbia avuto
che noi abbiamo avuto

PAST PERFECT
che io avessi avuto
che tu avessi avuto
che lui/lei/Lei avesse avuto
che noi avessimo avuto

che voi abbiate avuto   *che voi aveste avuto*
che loro abbiano avuto   *che loro avessero avuto*

IMPERATIVE

PRESENT
abbi (tu)
abbia (Lei)
abbiamo (noi)
abbiate (voi)
abbiano (Loro)

CONDITIONAL

PRESENT
io avrei
tu avresti
lui/lei/Lei avrebbe
noi avremmo
voi avreste
loro avrebbero

PERFECT
io avrei avuto
tu avresti avuto
lui/lei/Lei avrebbe avuto
noi avremmo avuto
voi avreste avuto
loro avrebbero avuto

INFINITIVE

PRESENT
avere

PERFECT
avere avuto

PARTICIPLES

PRESENT
avente

PERFECT
avuto

GERUND

PRESENT
avendo

PERFECT
avendo avuto

44. SOME IRREGULAR VERBS

(Only irregular tenses are indicated. Other tenses follow the regular pattern of the conjugation as shown in the tenses of the verb.)

Andare = to go
Ind. pres.: *vado, vai, va, andiamo, andate, vanno.*
Future: *andrò, andrai, andrà, andremo, andrete, andranno.*
Subj. pres.: *vada, vada, vada, andiamo, andiate, vadano.*
Imperative: *va', vada, andiamo, andate, vadano.*
Cond. pres.: *andrei, andresti, andrebbe, andremmo, andreste, andrebbero.*
Past part.: *andato.*

Bere = to drink
Ind. pres.: *bevo, bevi, beve, beviamo, bevete, bevono.*
Imperfect: *bevevo, bevevi,* etc.
Preterit: *bevvi, bevesti, bevve, bevemmo, beveste, bevvero.*
Future: *berrò, berrai, berra, berremo, berrete, berrano.*
Subj. imp.: *bevessi, bevessi, bevesse, bevessimo, beveste, bevessero.*
Cond. pres.: *berrei, berresti, berrebbe, berremmo, berreste, berrebbero.*
Past part.: *bevuto.*

Cadere = to fall
Future: *cadrò, cadrai, cadrà, cadremo, cadrete, cadranno.*
Preterit: *caddi, cadesti, cadde, cademmo, cadeste, caddero.*
Cond. pres.: *cadrei, cadresti, cadrebbe, cadremmo, cadreste, cadrebbero.*
Past part.: *caduto/-a*

Chiedere = to ask
Preterit: *chiesi, chiedesti, chiese, chiedemmo, chiedeste, chiesero.*
Past part.: *chiesto.*

Chiudere = to shut
Preterit: *chiusi, chiudesti, chiuse, chiudemmo, chiudeste, chiusero.*
Past part.: *chiuso.*

Conoscere = to know
Preterit: *conobbi, conoscesti, conobbe, conoscemmo, conosceste, conobbero.*
Past part.: *conosciuto.*

Cuocere = to cook
Ind. pres.: *cuocio, cuoci, cuoce, cociamo, cocete, cuociono.*
Preterit: *cossi, cocesti, cosse, cocemmo, coceste, cossero.*
Subj. pres.: *cuocia* or *cuoca, cuocia/cuoca, cuocia/cuoca, c(u)ociamo, c(u)ociate, cuociano.*
Imperative: *cuoci, cuoc(i)a, c(u)ociamo, c(u)ociete, cuoc(i)ano.*
Past part.: *cotto.*

Dare = to give
Ind. pres.: *do, dai, dà, diamo, date, danno.*
Preterit: *diedi* or *detti, desti, diede* or *dette, demmo, deste, dettero* or *diedero.*
Subj. pres.: *dia, dia, dia, diamo, diate, diano.*
Subj. imper.: *dessi, dessi, desse, dessimo, deste, dessero.*
Imperative: *da', dia, diamo, date, diano.*
Past part.: *dato.*

Dire = to say
Ind. pres.: *dico, dici, dice, diciamo, dite, dicono.*
Imperfect: *dicevo, dicevi, diceva, dicevamo, dicevate, dicevano.*
Preterit: *dissi, dicesti, disse, dicemmo, diceste, dissero.*
Subj. pres.: *dica, dica, dica, diciamo, diciate, dicano.*
Subj. imper.: *dicessi, dicessi, dicesse, dicessimo, diceste, dicessero.*

Imperative: *di, dica, diciamo, dite, dicano*.
Past part.: *detto*.

Dovere = to owe, to be obliged, to have to
Ind. pres.: *devo* or *debbo, devi, deve, dobbiamo,* or *dovete, devono,* or *debbono*.
Future: *dovrò, dovrai, dovrà, dovremo, dovrete, dovranno*.
Subj. pres.: *deva* or *debba, deva* or *debba, deva* or *debba, dobbiamo, dobbiate, devano* or *debbano*.
Cond. pres.: *dovrei, dovresti, dovrebbe, dovremmo, dovreste, dovrebbero*.
Past part.: *dovuto*.

Fare = to do
Ind. pres.: *faccio, fai, fa, facciamo, fate, fanno*.
Imperfect: *facevo, facevi, faceva, facevamo, facevate, facevano*.
Preterit: *feci, facesti, fece, facemmo, faceste, fecero*.
Subj. pres.: *faccia, faccia, faccia, facciamo, facciate, facciano*.
Subj. imp.: *facessi, facessi, facesse, facessimo, faceste, facessero*.
Imper. pres.: *fa', faccia, facciamo, fate, facciano*.
Past part.: *fatto*.

Leggere = to read
Preterit: *lessi, leggesti, lesse, leggemo, leggeste, lessero*.
Past part.: *letto*.

Mettere = to put
Preterit: *misi, mettesti, mise, mettemmo, metteste, misero*.
Past part.: *messo*.

Morire = to die
Ind. pres.: *muoio, muori, muore, moriamo, morite, muoiono*.
Future: *morirò* or *morrò, mor(i)rai, mor(i)rà, mor(i)remo, mor(i)rete, mor(i)ranno*.

Subj. pres.: *muoia, muoia, muoia, moriamo, moriate, muoiano.*
Cond. pres.: *morirei* or *morrei, mor(i)resti, mor(i)rebbe, mor(i)remmo, mor(i)reste, mor(i)rebbero.*
Past part.: *morto.*

Nascere = to be born
Preterit: *nacqui, nascesti, nacque, nascemmo, nasceste, nacquero.*
Past part.: *nato.*

Piacere = to please, to like
Ind. pres.: *piaccio, piaci, piace, piacciamo, piacete, piacciono.*
Preterit: *piacqui, piacesti, piacque, piacemmo, piaceste, piacquero.*
Subj. pres.: *piaccia, piaccia, piaccia, piac(c)iamo, piac(c)iate, piacessero.*
Past part.: *piaciuto.*

Piovere = to rain
Preterit: *piovve, piovvero.*
Past part.: *piovuto.*

Potere = to be able, can
Ind. pres.: *posso, puoi, può, possiamo, potete, possono.*
Future: *potrò, potrai, potrà, potremo, potrete, potranno.*
Subj. pres.: *possa, possa, possa, possiamo, possiate, possano.*
Cond. pres.: *potrei, portresti, potrebbe, potremmo, potreste, potrebbero.*
Past part.: *potuto*

Ridere = to laugh
Preterit: *risi, ridesti, rise, ridemmo, rideste, risero.*
Past part.: *riso.*

Rimanere = to stay

Ind. pres.: *rimango, rimani, rimane, rimaniamo, rimanete, rimangono.*

Preterit: *rimasi, rimanesti, rimase, rimanemmo, rimaneste, rimasero.*

Future: *rimarrò, rimarrai, rimarrà, rimarremo, rimarrete, rimarranno.*

Subj. pres.: *rimanga, rimanga, rimanga, rimaniamo, rimaniate, rimangano.*

Cond. pres.: *rimarrei, rimarresti, rimarrebbe, rimarremmo, rimarreste, rimarrebbero.*

Past part.: *rimasto.*

Rispondere = to answer

Preterit: *risposi, rispondesti, rispose, rispondemmo, rispondeste, risposero.*

Past part.: *risposto.*

Salire = to go up, to climb

Ind. pres.: *salgo, sali, sale, saliamo, salite, salgono.*

Subj. pres.: *salga, salga, salga, saliamo, saliate, salgano.*

Imperative: *sali, salga, saliamo, salite, salgano.*

Past part.: *salito.*

Sapere = to know

Ind. pres.: *so, sai, sa, sappiamo, sapete, sanno.*

Future: *saprò, saprai, saprà, sapremo, saprete, sapranno.*

Preterit: *seppi, sapesti, seppe, sapemmo, sapeste, seppero.*

Subj. pres.: *sappia, sappia, sappia, sappiamo, sappiate, sappiano.*

Imperative: *sappi, sappia, sappiamo, sappiate, sappiano.*

Cond. pres.: *saprei, sapresti, saprebbe, sapremmo, sapreste, saprebbero.*

Past part.: *saputo.*

Scegliere = to choose, select
Ind. pres.: *scelgo, scegli, sceglie, scegliamo, scegliete, scelgono.*
Preterit: *scelsi, scegliesti, scelse, scegliemmo, sceglieste, scelsero.*
Subj. pres.: *scelga, scelga, scelga, scegliamo, scegliate, scelgano.*
Imperative: *scegli, scelga, scegliamo, scegliete, scelgano.*
Past part.: *scelto.*

Scendere = to go down, descend
Preterit: *scesi, scendeste, scese, scendemmo, scendeste, scesero.*
Past part.: *sceso.*

Scrivere = to write
Preterit: *scrissi, scrivesti, scrisse, scrivemmo, scriveste, scrissero.*
Past part.: *scritto.*

Sedere = to sit
Ind. pres.: *siedo, siedi, siede, sediamo, sedete, siedono.*
Subj. pres.: *sieda, sieda, sieda, sediamo, sediate, siedano.*
Imperative: *siedi, sieda, sediamo, sedete, siedano.*
Past part.: *seduto*

Stare = to stay; to remain (to be)
Ind. pres.: *sto, stai, sta, stiamo, state, stanno.*
Preterit: *stetti, stesti, stette, stemmo, steste, stettero.*
Future: *starò, starai, starà, staremo, starete, staranno.*
Subj. pres.: *stia, stia, stia, stiamo, stiate, stiano.*
Subj. imper.: *stessi, stessi, stesse, stessimo, steste, stessero.*
Imperative: *sta', stia, stiamo, stiate, stiano.*
Cond. pres.: *starei, staresti, starebbe, staremmo, stareste, starebbero.*
Past part.: *stato.*

Uscire = to go out
Ind. pres.: *esco, esci, esce, usciamo, uscite, escono.*
Subj. pres.: *esca, esca, esca, usciamo, usciate, escano.*
Imperative: *esci, esca, usciamo, uscite, escano.*
Past part.: *uscito*

Vedere = to see
Ind. pres.: *vedo, vedi, vede, vediamo, vedete, vedono.*
Preterit: *vidi, vedesti, vide, vedemmo, vedeste, videro.*
Future: *vedrò, vedrai, vedrà, vedremo, vedrete, vedranno.*
Past part.: *visto* or *veduto.*

Venire = to come
Ind. pres.: *vengo, vieni, viene, veniamo, venite, vengono.*
Preterit: *venni, venisti, venne, venimmo, veniste, vennero.*
Future: *verrò, verrai, verrà, verremo, verrete, verranno.*
Subj. pres.: *venga, venga, venga, veniamo, veniate, vengano.*
Imperative: *vieni, venga, veniamo, venite, vengano.*
Cond. pres.: *verrei, verresti, verrebbe, verremmo, verreste,*
  verrebbero.
Pres. part.: *veniente.*
Past part.: *venuto.*

Vivere = to live
Preterit: *vissi, vivesti, visse, vivemmo, viveste, vissero.*
Future: *vivrò, vivrai, vivrà, vivremo, vivrete, vivranno.*
Cond. pres.: *vivrei, vivresti, vivrebbe, vivremmo, vivreste,*
  vivrebbero.
Past part.: *vissuto.*

Volere = to want
Ind. pres.: *voglio, vuoi, vuole, vogliamo, volete, vogliono.*
Preterit: *volli, volesti, volle, volemmo, voleste, vollero.*
Future: *vorrò, vorrai, vorrà, vorremo, vorrete, vorranno.*

Subj. pres.: *voglia, voglia, voglia, vogliamo, vogliate, vogliano*.

Cond. pres.: *vorrei, vorresti, vorrebbe, vorremmo, vorreste, vorrebbero*.

Past part.: *voluto*.

LETTER WRITING

A. FORMAL INVITATIONS AND ACCEPTANCES
INVITI FORMALI

marzo 2002

Il signore e la signora Peretti hanno il piacere di annunciare il matrimonio della loro figlia Maria con il signor Giovanni Rossi, ed hanno il piacere di invitarvi alla cerimonia che avrà luogo nella Chiesa di San Giuseppe, il sei di questo mese, alle ore dodici. Dopo la cerimonia un ricevimento sarà dato in onore degli sposi nella casa dei genitori della sposa.

March 2002

Mr. and Mrs. Peretti take pleasure in announcing the wedding of their daughter Maria to Mr. Giovanni Rossi, and have the pleasure of inviting you to the ceremony, which will take place at the Church of San Giuseppe on the sixth of this month at twelve noon. There will be a reception for the newlyweds afterward at the residence of the bride's parents.

---

settembre 2002

Il signore e la signora De Marchi hanno il piacere di invitare il signor Rossi e la sua gentile signora a cena lunedì prossimo, alle otto.

September 2002

Mr. and Mrs. De Marchi take pleasure in inviting Mr. and Mrs. Rossi to dinner next Monday at eight o'clock.

---

marzo 2002

Il signore e la signora Martini hanno il piacere di invitare il signore e la signora Parisi al ricevimento in onore della loro figlia Anna, domenica sera, 19 marzo, alle ore nove.

March 2002

Mr. and Mrs. Martini take pleasure in inviting Mr. and Mrs. Parisi to a party in honor of their daughter Anna, on Sunday evening, March 19, at nine o'clock.

RESPONSES
RISPOSTE

Il signor Parisi e signora ringraziano per il cortese invito, felici di prendere parte al ricevimento del 19 marzo p.v.

Thank you for your kind invitation. We will be honored to attend the reception on March 19th.

[Note: *p.v.* = *prossimo venturo,* which means "the next coming" (month). *c.m.* = *corrente mese,* which means "of this month" (the running month.)]

I coniugi Rossi accettano il gentile invito per lunedì prossimo e ringraziano sentitamente.

Mr. and Mrs. Rossi will be honored to have dinner with Mr. and Mrs. De Marchi next Monday. With kindest regards.

I coniugi Rossi ringraziano sentitamente il signore e la signora Peretti per il cortese invito, spiacenti che impegni precedenti non permettano loro di poter accettare.

Mr. and Mrs. Rossi thank Mr. and Mrs. Peretti for their kind invitation and regret that they are unable to come due to a previous engagement.

B.   THANK-YOU NOTES
BIGLIETTI DI RINGRAZIAMENTO

Roma, 5 marzo 2002

Cara Anna,

Poche righe soltanto per sapere come stai e per ringraziarti del bellissimo vaso che mi hai regalato. L'ho messo sul pianoforte, e ti assicuro che è bellissimo.

Spero di vederti il mese prossimo al ricevimento di Angela. Sono sicura che la festa sarà molto divertente.

Mi auguro che la tua famiglia stia bene, come la mia. Ti saluto affettuosamente.

Maria

March 5, 2002

Dear Anna,

Just a few lines to say hello and also to let you know that I received the beautiful vase you sent me as a gift. I've put it on the piano, and you can't imagine how nice it looks.

I hope to see you at Angela's party next month. I think it's going to be a lot of fun.

I hope your family is all well, as is mine. Everyone here is fine.

Affectionately,

Maria

C. BUSINESS LETTERS
LETTERE COMMERCIALI

Cavatorta & Co.,
Via Veneto 125,
Roma—Italia

Ditta Marini e Figli
Via Nomentana, 11
Roma.

Roma, 2 aprile 2002

Gentili Signori:

Abbiamo il piacere di presentarvi il portatore di questa lettera, signor Carlo Fontanesi, che è uno dei nostri agenti attualmente in visita alle principali città del vostro paese. Inutile aggiungere che qualsiasi gentilezza sarà usata al signor Fontanesi sarà da noi gradita come un personale favore.

Ringraziandovi in anticipo, vi inviamo i nostri distinti saluti.

Cavatorta & Co.
il Presidente

Cavatorta & Co.
Via Veneto 125
Rome—Italy

(Firm) Marini & Sons
Via Nomentana, 11
Rome

April 2, 2002

Gentlemen:

We have the pleasure of introducing to you the bearer of this letter, Mr. Carlo Fontanesi, one of our salesmen, who is visiting the principal cities of your country. Needless to add, we shall greatly appreciate any courtesy you extend to him. (It is needless to say to you that we shall consider any courtesy you extend to him as a personal favor.)

Thanking you in advance, we send our best regards.

Cavatorta & Co.
President

Milano, 3 marzo 2002
Signor Giulio Perri
direttore di "Il Mondo"
Via Montenapoleone, 3
Milano.

Gentile Signore:

   Includo un assegno di ¶100 (cento) per un anno di abbonamento alla sua rivista.

Distintamente

Lucia Landi

Lucia Landi
Corso Vittorio Emanuele, 8
Roma

March 3, 2002

Mr. Giulio Perri
Editor of *Il Mondo*
Via Montenapoleone, 3
Milan

Dear Sir:
   Enclosed please find a check for 100 euros for a year's subscription to your magazine.

Very truly yours,
Lucia Landi

Lucia Landi
8 Corso Vittorio Emanuele
Rome

D. INFORMAL LETTERS
LETTERE INFORMALI

Caro Giuseppe,

   Sono stato molto lieto di ricevere la tua ultima lettera. Prima di tutto desidero darti la grande notizia. Ho final- mente deciso di fare un viaggio a Roma, dove intendo rimanere tutto il mese di maggio. Anna verrà con me. Lei è molto felice che avrà così l'occasione di conoscervi. Cerca, perciò, di essere possibilmente libero, per allora.

   Gli affari vanno bene e spero che il buon vento continui. L'altro giorno ho visto Antonio e lui mi ha chiesto tue notizie.

   Ti sarei grato se vorrai riservarci una camera all'albergo Nazionale. Scrivi presto. Saluti ad Elena.

tuo
Giovanni

Dear Giuseppe,

   I was very happy to get your last letter. First of all, let me give you the big news. I have finally decided to make a trip to Rome, where I expect to spend all of May. Anna will come with me. She is extremely happy to be able to meet the two of you at last. Try therefore to be as free as you can then.

   Business is good now, and I hope will keep that way (that the good wind will continue). I saw Antonio the other day and he asked me about you.

   I'd be grateful to you if you would try to reserve a room for us at the National Hotel. Write soon. Give my regards to Helen.

Yours,
Giovanni

E. E-MAILS

a. A business e-mail

Gentile Giovanni Maria,

grazie per aver acquistato su mondowind online.
Abbiamo ricevuto l'ordine che hai effettuato presso mondowind on line.
Ecco il dettaglio del tuo acquisto:
1 Ricarica ReWind on line da 60 euro
per il numero 320-7757155
Controlla che i dati riportati siano esatti, annota il numero dell'ordine e conservalo per qualsiasi verifica.
Puoi anche verificare lo stato di avanzamento del tuo ordine, aggiornato in tempo reale, direttamente sul sito, cliccando sul link 'Tracking ordine' posto a sinistra.
Riceverai presto aggiornamenti sullo stato del tuo acquisto.

Cordiali saluti,
Servizio Clienti mondowind online

Dear Giovanni Maria,

Thanks for shopping on mondowind online.

We received your order. Here are the details of your purchase:

1 Richarge ReWind on line for 60 euros

for number 320-775-7155

Please check that this information is correct, make a note of the order number and keep it for any check.

You can also verify the status of your order, updated in real time, directly on the site, by clicking on the link "Tracking Order" on your left.

You'll soon receive updates on the status of your purchase.

Sincerely,
Customer services mondowind online

b. A personal e-mail

Carissima, grazie dell' e-mail! Buone vacanze anche a te! Ti mando in allegato la foto del mio nuovo cane. Inoltrala anche a Fabio. Grazie! A presto! Carla

Dearest, thanks a lot for your e-mail! Happy Holidays to you too! I'm sending in attachment the picture of my new dog. Forward it to Fabio too. Thank you! See you soon! Carla

F. FORMS OF SALUTATIONS

Formal

Signore	Sir
Signora	Madam (Mrs.)
Signorina	Miss
Professore	My dear Professor

Gentile Signor Rossi	My dear Mr. Rossi
Gentile Signora Rossi	My dear Mrs. Rossi
Gentile Signorina Rossi	My dear Miss Rossi

Informal

Caro Antonio	My dear Antonio
Cara Anna	My dear Anna
Carissimo Paolo	Dearest Paolo
Carissima Giovanna	Dearest Giovanna
Ciao, tesoro	My dearest

G. FORMS OF COMPLIMENTARY CLOSINGS

Formal

1. *Distinti saluti.* — Very truly yours.

2. *Cordiali saluti.* — Sincerely. (Heartfelt feelings.)

3. *Le invio cordiali saluti.* — Sincerely. (I send you heartfelt greetings.)

Informal

1. *In attesa di vostre notizie vi invio i miei sinceri e cordiali saluti.* — Best regards. (Waiting for your news, I send you my sincere and heartfelt greetings.)

2. *Sperando di ricevere presto tue notizie ti invio cordialissimi saluti.* — Best regards. (Hoping to hear from you soon, I send you my most heartfelt greetings.)

3. *Cari saluti.* — Best.

4. *Un abbraccio.*   Love. (Hugs.)

5. *Un bacio(ne).*   Kisses.

6. *A presto.*   Talk to you soon.

H. FORMS OF THE ENVELOPE

Paolo Bolla
Via Veneto, 10
00100 Roma

        Gent.mo Sig.
        Angelo Rossi
        Piazza Roma, 24
        80133 Napoli

Barbara Soldi
Via Nomentana, 27
00100 Roma

        Gent.ma Sig.ra
        Marcella Marini
        Via Montenapoleone, 13
        20100 Milano

Anna Rossi
Piazza Vittorio Emanuele, 9
50123 Firenze

        Gent.ma Sig.na
        Silvana Tarri
        Piazza Venezia, 71
        00100 Roma

INTERNET RESOURCES

The following is a list of useful websites for those students who would like to enhance their language-learning experience.

Italian Government Tourist Board
www.italiantourism.com

Events, food, sport
www.allaboutitaly.com

Events, accommodations, and general information
www.initaly.com

Information on all of Italy
www.discoveritalia.com

Museums of Italy
www.museionline.com

Rome
www.romaturismo.com

Florence
www.firenze.net

Venice
www.turismovenezia.it

Amalfi Coast
www.touristbureau.com/indexIta.asp

Sicily
www.bestofsicily.com

Italian newspaper from Milan
www.corriere.it

The Italian version of Yahoo!
it.yahoo.com